Dainty Dress Diaries

CATHERINE CARTON is the lady behind the award-winning interiors and lifestyle blog daintydressdiaries.com. She is a lover of upcycling, recycling and making the old new again.

Dainty Dress Diaries was created in 2014. While brain-dumping potential names with a workmate, Catherine and her pal decided to go with 'Dainty' because Catherine is 4'11", 'Dress' because all she wore was cute dresses, and 'Diaries' so that the blog could cover a wide range of topics.

In the beginning, Catherine mostly blogged about vintage style, fashion and homeware, but over the years she has become known for her warm personality and the unique creative projects she shares with her online community.

www.daintydressdiaries.com

www.youtube.com/daintydiaries

www.instagram.com/daintydressdiaries

Dainty Dress Diaries

50 beautiful
home-crafting projects
to awaken your
creativity

Catherine Carton

THE O'BRIEN PRESS
DUBLIN

First published 2022 by The O'Brien Press Ltd.,
12 Terenure Road East, Rathgar, Dublin 6, D06 HD27, Ireland.
Tel: +353 1 4923333. Fax: +353 1 4922777
Email: books@obrien.ie. Website: obrien.ie
The O'Brien Press is a member of Publishing Ireland.

ISBN 978-1-78849-296-6

10 9 8 7 6 5 4 3 2 1
26 25 24 23 22

Printed by L&C Printing Group, Poland.
The paper in this book is produced using pulp from managed forests.

This is a DIY book, and all projects involve a degree of risk. Every effort has been
made to ensure that all the information in this book is accurate. However, since
conditions, tools, materials and skills will vary, the publisher and author cannot
be responsible for any injury, loss or damage that may result from the use of the
information in this book.

Published in

In loving memory of my dad,

Patrick,

With love

I have so many people who I want to express gratitude to for helping me along this journey.

It takes a village to create a book, so firstly, I want to thank all the team at The O'Brien Press for bringing this book to life. A special thank you to my editor Nicola, who made sure we dotted our i's and crossed our t's and patiently pieced this project together, and to Harri and Prin for their extra proofreading help. A big thank you to Emma for beautifully designing this book and making the pages come to life, and to Eoin for his lovely illustrations. To the OBP sales and publicity team for getting this book in many places and on as many shelves as possible.

Thank you to all my family for their continued support throughout the years. My mam, brothers, niece and nephew, thank you for the giggles along the way.

Thank you to my close tribe of women who cheer me on, who listen and hold space for me to grow. Thank you for being there through every win and every wobble. An extra special thank you to Karen, Joanne, Rachel and Adele.

Last but not least, thank you to the online community, who support me daily. Whether it is a loving comment, sharing feedback or giving ideas, I am forever grateful for your help and encouragement.

Go raibh míle maith agaibh

Contents

Introduction

What do you think of when you hear the word 'creativity'? The dictionary would say it's the use of imagination or original ideas to create something; inventiveness. But I think it's more than that. I believe creativity has the power to change our lives and to heal us too.

When I was in my twenties, I was lucky enough to purchase my own house. There wasn't much cash left in the kitty, so I began upcycling, recycling and using whatever I had to create my dream home – which led me to start sharing my projects on a blog, Dainty Dress Diaries. I put my hand to almost every material and tool you can think of. The thing with creativity is, once you start, you can't stop! As Maya Angelou said, 'You can't use up creativity. The more you use, the more you have.'

Getting crafty is fun, but it's also a healthy distraction during tough times. Whenever I have moments of uncertainty or when I feel overwhelmed, picking up a paintbrush or a needle and thread takes me away from my worries. It seems like such a simple thing, refreshing a piece of furniture or sewing a cushion, but there is a feeling of joy and satisfaction and accomplishment; pride in making something new or transforming something old.

When we allow ourselves to create, our minds open up to ideas in other areas of our lives too. In this digital age, there is so much noise that it's becoming harder and harder to just be still. We are constantly plugged into our devices, reacting to every beep. It's so healing to hit the do-not-disturb button, to carve out some time for creativity and inner peace.

But I'm not a creative person, I hear you say! The magic of creativity is, you never lose it. As kids, we are naturally curious. We question things, and we seek out wonder. We don't care what others think or what the end product is going to be – we create for the sake of it, no perfection, just play. Remember in junior infants, when you had ten minutes to play in the Wendy house before lessons? You had a burst of energy, a moment to clear the head before you sat down to learn. Why did that stop? And can we get it back?

But why bother trying, you ask, if it won't be perfect? Lots of us suffer from perfection paralysis and are too afraid to start creating for fear that we won't do it 'right'. Social media doesn't help, but

remember not to compare your beginning to someone else's middle. On my blog you'll see the final results of my projects – believe me when I say there were plenty of mistakes along the way! And this book was once a badly written first draft, but now it is in your hands. Fall in love with a beginner's mindset, unplug from the noise and create just for you. Release your attachment to the outcome, and that's when the magic will happen.

There are many ways to get creative, from photography and baking and painting to gardening and sewing. Throughout this book, I'll suggest some ways to reignite your creativity. Some ideas you will use, some you won't – follow the ones that light you up.

My blog, Dainty Dress Diaries, is my home on the internet, and I love sharing my projects and experiences there. Looking back through the Dainty archives, I am proud of the girl who was brave enough to simply begin. I am bursting with joy to create this book and have all my favourite projects in one place for you. So now I ask you to get lost inside the pages, be inspired, create and play.

Catherine

Chapter One

Crafternoons and the Power of Pause

I love nothing more than putting my phone on silent and taking an afternoon to craft. It's a way to flex my creative muscles and try something new, but also a lovely opportunity for a few hours of mindfulness.

In this chapter, I will share projects that are straightforward, don't require a huge amount of equipment, and can be achieved by yourself over an afternoon. They'll give you the creative buzz that I talk so much about, and you will be beaming with pride when you tell others, 'I made that!'

We have so many distractions at our fingertips these days that it can be hard to think for ourselves. We feel a need to react instantly to things we see, snapping photos or posting or searching for information, because the devices in our hands have us trained that way.

Whenever I feel upset, triggered or anxious, I try to hit pause. I gather my supplies, switch everything off, and give myself an hour or two to play. Maybe it's the activity of doing something completely different, but my anxiety eases, the overwhelming thoughts shrink, and I feel grounded again and better able to respond to the world around me.

Rose-Scented Melt-and-Pour Soaps

Making soap is a perfect way to spend an afternoon, and it leaves your home smelling delicious. There are many ways to do it – this is an easy one. We will use a melt-and-pour soap base, which is handy for beginners as you don't need to get caught up with cure time or measuring chemicals.

You can buy melt-and-pour soap bases online or from a craft shop, then you just add some essential oil, or a mixture of different oils, to create your perfect blend.

Here, I'm using rose essential oil, which is known to soothe and moisturise, making it perfect for dry hands. I also add dried rose petals to my soap, but this is optional. There are loads of soap recipes you can try if you are not a fan of rose; aloe vera, lavender and lemon balm, and orange and cinnamon are also popular blends.

What you need

Saucepan
Heat-resistant glass jug or bowl ★
Melt-and-pour soap base
Spatula ★
Rose essential oil
Soap colourant (optional)
Silicone mould ★
Dried rose petals (optional)

*★ Keep these for soap-making only –
not to be reused for cooking*

- Create a double boiler by heating water in a saucepan and adding a glass jug or bowl on top. Break the large block of soap base into smaller chunks and add them to your jug or bowl. I'm using a goats milk base here, but you could also choose soy, shea butter, etc.
- Melt your soap base in the double boiler, stirring with the spatula until it has melted into a liquid. You can also melt the base in the microwave in thirty-second intervals, stirring in between.
- Once the mixture is nice and smooth, take it off the heat and add in the essential oil. I used 20 drops of rose oil to 400ml of melted soap base.
- Most soap bases are clear or white, so if you decide to use colorant – as I have done, to give my soaps a rosy-pink hue – add it in now, stirring between each drop until you get the colour you want.

- Place your soap moulds on a baking tray to avoid spillage. I've chosen a rose-shaped mould, but you could also go for a classic square. Pour the mixture into each mould.
- You can now add dried rose petals into the soap. I love the extra texture the petals give, but please note that the natural colourants can cause some discolouration.
- I always leave my soaps to set overnight, but they usually harden within an hour or two. If you notice bubbles on the backs of your soap, you can use a little rubbing alcohol to stop them forming.
- Melt-and-pour soap bases contain lye, so once they have hardened the curing process is complete, and you can begin using your lovely new homemade soaps.

If you're gifting your soap, note down on a sticker or label what ingredients you've used as some people's skin can be irritated by certain essential oils.

Clay Leaf Trinket Bowl

One of my favourite things to do is to play with clay. It reminds me of junior infants, when you had a scrap of lino and some modelling clay and your imagination! Well, air-dry clay is just as fun, less messy, and your creations will be permanent.

Air-dry clay can take about twenty-four hours to harden, but if you're less patient you can choose oven-bake clay. They're both available from craft shops and online, and even in some pound shops.

These adorable trinket dishes look cute on the nightstand and are perfect for popping your jewellery in. No two are the same, so they make a very special gift for friends and family.

What you need

Air-dry clay
A leaf
A rolling pin ★ or a smooth bottle
A craft knife
Recycled plastic wrap
A dessert bowl
Acrylic paint
A paintbrush
Clear varnish or PVA glue (optional)

★ *Not to be reused for cooking*

- When picking a leaf, choose one that is nice and wide as this will give you a stronger dish. You can also use a leaf from a houseplant. Try to find one that is not damaged.
- Grab a handful of clay, place it on a tablemat or other protective surface, and roll it out using your rolling pin. Don't make it too thin, as it may break after hardening.
- Place the leaf in the centre of the clay. Then, using your rolling pin, lightly roll the leaf to transfer the details into the clay.
- Using a craft knife, cut the excess clay off to leave the shape of the leaf. You can use a small amount of water and your finger to smooth any rough edges.
- Use some recycled plastic wrap to cover the inside of the bowl. Lay the clay leaf inside to give it a curved shape. Allow your clay to harden overnight in the bowl.

- If you find it's taking longer, pop it near a radiator or a sunny window. As your clay dries, it will lighten in colour.
- Now the fun part! Use whatever paint you have lying around to paint your clay leaves. If doing this craft with children, I recommend acrylic. You can also use chalk paint or spray paint – I used a bright-copper metallic spray. You will notice all the details from the leaf start to become visible when you apply paint. Use as many coats as you like, but two are usually enough.
- An optional step is to apply a coat of clear varnish (matt or satin finish) or a layer of PVA glue. This will protect your trinket dishes and make them easier to clean.
- Allow your paint or varnish to fully dry before styling your un-be-leaf-able dishes as you please.

Sweet Nights Pillow Spray

I always try to switch off and wind down before bed. In a world where our attention is constantly drawn in different directions, from smartphone pings to family demands, it's no wonder we are all a little frazzled by evening time. I try not to look at screens for an hour or more before bedtime, and I do some meditation to slow my mind.

I also love to spritz my pillow with fragrance. You can buy all sorts of pillow sprays these days, but it's so easy to make a batch of your own, in your own favourite blend. It's not a magic ingredient for a good night's sleep, but as part of a bedtime routine, a pillow spray with essential oils can be wonderfully relaxing. Below is my favourite recipe, which will make around 60 ml.

What you need

A funnel
A reusable spray bottle, preferably amber glass
Distilled water (40 ml)
One tablespoon (15 ml) of witch hazel
30 drops of lavender essential oil
15 drops of ylang-ylang essential oil
7 drops of frankincense essential oil
5 drops of cedarwood essential oil

- Using the funnel to prevent spillage, add the distilled water to your glass bottle, followed by the witch hazel, which will help the oils to mix.

- Next, add in your essential oils. You can adapt the recipe above to your own preferences. Some people like a simple lavender pillow spray, as lavender is known to help ease anxiety and insomnia.

- Give the bottle a shake, then lightly mist your pillow. I like to give it two or three spritzes.

- These pillow sprays make an ideal gift! Remember to list the ingredients on a label so the receiver knows what's inside.

> It's a good idea to do a patch test with each essential oil to make sure you're not sensitive or allergic to it before making your pillow mist. Try to find high-quality oil created sustainably, and check that it's an essential oil rather than a fragrance oil.

Craffernoons and the Power of Pause   21

Mercury Glass Effect Vases

Did you have mercury glass baubles on your Christmas tree as a kid? Also known as silvered glass or poor man's silver, mercury glass was an inexpensive alternative to silver that was used in wealthy homes back in the 1800s. It's become popular again of late, especially for wedding decor.

While you can easily pick up vintage mercury glass pieces for your home, they can be expensive. Let me share how you can create the same effect, turning old glassware into antique-looking vases using just spray paint and vinegar.

What you need

Glassware
A spray bottle
Water
White vinegar
Protective gloves
Mirror-effect spray paint
Tissue or kitchen paper

- Choose glasses that are different heights and shapes. You can use any size, but a wider glass will be easier, as you can fit your hand inside when blotting the paint.
- The first thing to do is clean your glass with warm, soapy water to remove any grease or finger marks.
- Add a 50/50 mixture of water and vinegar to your spray bottle. (If you have any left over at the end of the project, it makes an excellent DIY window cleaner.)
- It's best to use spray paint outdoors, but if you must work indoors, do it in a well-ventilated area like a garage or a shed. Before you start spraying, pop on your gloves. You can choose to spray the inside or the outside of the glass. If it's your first attempt, it might be easier to spray the outside.
- First, lightly mist the glass with the water and vinegar mix. Then spray one coat of mirror spray paint. Using a tissue or kitchen paper, dab any water spots on the glass very lightly, taking care not to rub the paint.
- Repeat the step above two or three more times to get your desired effect, then let your vase fully dry and cure.
- You can style your vases with real or faux flowers or just leave them empty. They're very popular in tablescapes and wedding displays.

Teacup Candles

I love a china teacup with a floral print! They're my guilty pleasure. I am forever collecting them in charity shops and on second-hand websites, and a great way to reuse them is by making teacup candles. They're easy and fun to create, perfect as gifts, and they give off a lovely warm glow as the candle burns. You can also use a china milk jug or sugar bowl – just make sure to check for any hairline cracks or damage.

The most popular waxes for candle-making are paraffin, soy and beeswax. Paraffin wax is the cheapest, but these days people often opt for natural waxes instead, especially ones that are ethically sourced. Below, I use a blend of lavender and lemongrass essential oils for my scented candles. If you are making these in Autumn, try the warm scent of ginger, cinnamon and clove.

What you need

Candle wax
A heat-resistant measuring jug ★
A saucepan
Candle thermometer
Essential oils
A metal spoon ★
China cups
Wicks
Glue (optional)
A coffee stirrer or wooden stick

★ *Not to be reused for cooking*

- The number of candles you'll end with depends on the size of your teacups, but you should get about two or three per 500 g of wax. Break up the wax and add it to your jug. Create a double boiler by heating water in a saucepan and adding the jug on top. Be careful not to let it overheat. Once the wax has melted, carefully take off the heat.

- If you are adding scent, use your candle thermometer to check the temperature of the melted wax before adding the oils, as if the wax is too cool, the oils may not mix evenly. The optimum temperature is between 85°C and 93°C (185°F and 200°F), depending on the type of wax you use.

- Natural essential oils are not as strong as synthetic fragrence oils, which means you will need to use more. I used roughly two teaspoons (10 ml) of essential oil per candle – or six teaspoons (30 ml) per 500 g batch – but this can go up or down, depending on the scent and your own personal taste.

- Stir your mixture with the spoon, and then it's ready to pour.

- Place your teacups on a tray or in the place they are going to sit overnight.

- Add a wick to the bottom of the cup. Most wicks will come with a small metal disc on the base. You can add a tiny bit of glue to the base and gently press it to the bottom of the cup.

- Before pouring your wax, place a stick across the top of the cup to centre the wick and keep it upright. Take extra care when pouring the hot wax and do it slowly so as not to dislodge the wick.

- I leave my candles out overnight to set, although some waxes cure quicker than others.

- Once the wax has hardened, trim your wick, leaving about an inch on top. If you notice any sinkholes, you can fix these by melting some fresh wax and doing a second pour. Sinkholes are common in candle-making, especially for beginners.

If it is your first time, I recommend doing a small batch to begin with; you can tweak each batch until they're perfect. Once your candles have burnt down, you can reuse the china cups for candle-making as many times as you like.

Flower Letters

There is nothing like getting a personalised gift or creating something bespoke for yourself. I originally made these for my baby niece's nursery, but they would be a fab wedding DIY too.

These floral letters can stand on a shelf, or you can put them inside a shadow box. Get creative with your choice of flowers, and you will have a unique and personal display for your home.

What you need

MDF wood letters
Paint (optional)
Hot glue gun or stronghold glue
Faux flowers and moss

These are a lovely, personalised gift for a newborn baby, but make sure they're displayed up high and out of reach of little hands.

- You can find wooden MDF letters in most craft stores and online. They come in various sizes and heights.

- I chose to paint my letters with some pink paint from an old tester pot, but you can also leave the natural wood for a rustic feel. Depending on the paint you use, you may need to apply two coats. Paint them all over, including the front, in case any wood shows under the moss.

- Faux flowers and moss work best for this DIY, as fresh won't last very long. Choose flowers that are not too large and think about the overall colour palette.

- If you plan to have your letters freestanding on a shelf, use lighter paper flowers and be careful not to overload. Test them as you go along to see if they're standing well. If the letters are to go in frames or a shadow box, you have more freedom.

- First, glue the moss in small sections using a hot glue gun or a stronghold glue. Avoid PVA glue for this project, as it takes longer to dry.

- Once the glue is dry, start on your flowers. It's a good idea to arrange them first, before gluing, as you can play around with the positioning. I added the larger flowers first and then went in with the smaller ones.

- Allow the letters to fully dry before displaying.

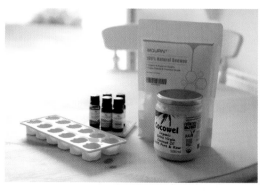

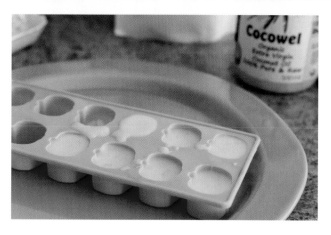

Pumpkin Spice Wax Melts

Do you ever find the scent of shop-bought wax melts too strong? Well, it's really easy to make your own, and you can tailor them to your own taste. For me, nothing says cosy season like the smell of pumpkin spice. Autumn is my favourite time of year, watching the leaves change colour and fall away; a gentle nudge from nature to remind us to allow other things in our lives to change and fall away too. I love warming my toes by the fire with a cat on my lap, and every time I smell these wax melts, it brings me back to that cosy autumn feeling.

What you need

Saucepan
Heat-resistant glass bowl
50 g of beeswax
100 g of coconut oil
30 drops of cinnamon bark essential oil
25 drops of ginger essential oil
15 drops of nutmeg essential oil
10 drops of clove essential oil
Silicone mould ★

★ Not to be reused for cooking

- Create a double boiler by heating water in a saucepan and adding a glass bowl on top. Once the water begins to boil, lower the temperature to allow it to simmer. Make sure to keep water in the pot, as it can evaporate over time.
- Add the beeswax and coconut oil. You can break up the beeswax before adding to make it easier to melt.
- When they have melted, add your essential oils. Stir well.
- Pour the mixture into your silicone mould and allow to set. I find that they harden quickly, but you can also put them in the fridge to move things along.
- Once fully set, gently remove the melts from your silicone mould.
- These wax melts give roughly four hours of burn time before the pumpkin spice scent dulls. However, you can add a few drops of essential oils to your melts to bring the scent back.
- To remove the melt from a wax burner, I light a tea light and hold it underneath; after a minute, the bottom of the wax melt will start to soften, and you can slide it out.

Découpaged Clothes Hanger

Découpage, which originated in France in the 17th Century, is simply the art of using paper cut-outs to decorate an item. You can use many different types of paper, from wallpaper and napkins to gold leaf, and decorate all sorts of items, from furniture to jewellery boxes or framed art.

I recommend starting with smaller projects – a tray, a mirror, a book, a photo frame or a tissue box – as it can be fiddly at first. Then, once you've built up your confidence, you can tackle bigger items like a vase, a lampshade or a chest of drawers. Here, we're going to decorate a wooden hanger.

What you need

A wooden hanger
A damp cloth
Découpage glue or PVA glue
Patterned paper or napkins
A soft, flat art brush
Clear varnish

- There are many types of découpage glue on the market, or you can use PVA glue. The specialist glues are easier to work with, while PVA takes longer to dry and can cause more wrinkles in the paper.

- When choosing paper, let your imagination run wild. You can use old postcards, photographs, decorative tissues, wallpaper and more. For beginners, I recommend tissue, as it is lightweight and manageable.

- First, wipe away any dust and dirt from your hanger, as the napkins will need a smooth, dry surface to stick to.

- Separate your napkins to leave you with the thinnest printed layer. Most napkins are three-ply, so make sure you get the thinnest piece.

- Apply a thin layer of glue to your hanger.

- Slowly place the napkin onto your hanger and gently brush it onto the surface. Start from the middle and brush outwards. Use a very gentle hand as napkins can tear easily, but if this happens, don't worry – you will be able to layer over any mistakes.

- If you get any wrinkles, just place a piece of cling film over your napkin and gently push them out with your finger. I find when using floral napkins, some wrinkles add to the texture of the flower.

- Layer your napkins around the wooden hanger until you are happy with the coverage.

- Allow the glue to dry, then apply a coat of clear varnish to seal your project, protect it from wear and make it wipeable. (Note: some découpage glues are self-sealing and will dry to a hardened finish.)

- Have fun finishing off your project with some embellishments, like a bow, a decorative trim or some jewels.

> To blend the napkin into the wood for a painted-on effect, lightly sand with fine-grit sandpaper when it is dry, taking care not to tear or lift the napkin.

Bouquet Boxes

Maybe it is my inner magpie, but I find it hard to part with a pretty box. You might be the same and have old accessory or hat boxes that you don't know what to do with. Floral bouquet boxes are popular these days, and here's an idea for creating your own, with an option for both fresh and faux flowers. These make beautiful gifts, but they also look lovely styled in your home.

The boxes I use here came with china tea sets. If you don't have anything to hand, you can pick up plain cardboard boxes from the craft shop and decorate them with patterned paper and bows. Other containers are fine too, like an old metal sweet tin or a wooden box. Have fun looking around your home to see what you can use.

What you need (faux)

A box of your choice
Polystyrene
Faux flowers
Gardening glove
A wire cutter
Ribbon or gift tag (optional)

What you need (fresh)

A box of your choice
Some plastic, like a used shopping bag
Tape or glue gun
Oasis foam
Fresh flowers
Ribbon or gift tag (optional)

Faux flower arrangement:

- Cut your polystyrene so it fits snugly in the bottom of your box.

- Using a wire cutter, carefully trim the stems on your faux flowers. Use a gardening glove to protect your hands.

- Arrange the faux flowers in the polystyrene. When making any floral arrangement, I work from the

middle outwards. Play around with the positioning of the flowers and go with what looks nice to you. Trust your eye!

• Add decorative ribbon to your box if you wish, or a gift tag.

Fresh flower arrangement:

• Fresh flowers need a drink, so we start by lining the box with plastic. A recycled shopping bag is perfect for this, as you won't see it when the flowers are inside. Check that there is no damage to your bag. Cut it to size and line the box, making sure it comes up to the rim. Use tape or a glue gun to secure it in place.

• Soak the floral oasis in water. Once it is moist, place it inside the box.

• Supermarket flowers are perfect for this DIY: roses, gypsophila, or any others that are in season. You can fill in gaps with foliage from your garden.

• Add decorative ribbon to your box if you wish, or a gift tag.

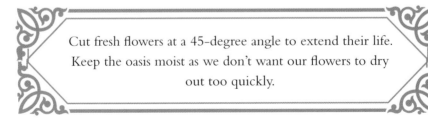

Cut fresh flowers at a 45-degree angle to extend their life.
Keep the oasis moist as we don't want our flowers to dry
out too quickly.

DIY Bath Shelf

I don't use my bath as much as I would like to, but when I do, I love to take a long soak and make a big deal about it! This bath shelf helps to create an at-home spa feel; it also gives you more storage and is handy for propping your phone up so you can watch a movie while you relax.

If this is your first foray into woodworking, don't worry – it's quite straightforward. You can use scrap pieces of wood and primary tools. If you don't feel confident cutting wood, some hardware shops will cut it for you.

What you need

A piece of wood
Two scrap pieces of wood
Measuring tape and pencil
A saw
Medium- and fine-grit sandpaper
Some screws and a drill, or wood glue
Paint, mixing bowl and dry cloth (optional)
Varnish
Decorative handles (optional)

- The first piece of wood will be the shelf itself. It should be around 1–2 in (2.5–5 cm) deep and 6–8 in (15–20 cm) wide. The length will be cut later to match the width of your bath – mine ended up being 26 in (66 cm).
- The two pieces of scrap wood will be used as bumpers for the underside of the shelf, to stop it from falling into the bath. They should be the same width as the shelf. Measure and cut these first.

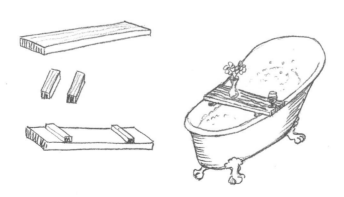

- Position your wood at a comfortable height on a table or a low sawhorse if you have one. Using a firm but gentle grip, start cutting. Let the saw do the work by using a smooth motion and long cuts. Try to avoid putting too much pressure on your saw, as this can cause the blade to buckle.
- Next, you'll cut the main shelf to size. Measure the width of your bath frame. Mine is 26 in (66 cm), but not all baths are a standard size. You want your piece of wood to be the same width as the bath frame, so mark with a pencil where you need to cut it.
- When the pieces are cut, smooth them using medium-grit sandpaper to soften the edges. Work your way up to fine-grit sandpaper for a smooth finish.
- To assemble the bath shelf, you will need a drill and some screws. Measure where you need your bumpers to go. The bumpers should sit on either end of the main piece of wood, with enough space so that they're inside the bathtub and not on the bathtub. Tip: Tape the bumpers on before screwing and place them on the bathtub. Once you are happy with the positioning, screw them into the main piece of wood.
- To stop the wood from splitting, drill pilot holes where you need the screws, then gently screw them in to secure the wood bumpers to the top piece of wood. Another option is to use wood glue for this stage, if you don't feel confident using a drill. When using wood glue, apply a generous amount of glue to the wood and clamp into place. Allow some extra time for the glue to dry.
- To bring out the details in my piece of timber, I whitewashed it. In a container, I mixed a 50/50 ratio of white paint to water and brushed this over my wood. I then used a dry cloth to wipe away the excess and work the whitewash into the grain of the wood. You can skip this step or use a wood stain if you prefer.
- To protect your wood from water damage, apply varnish. Make sure you choose a good-quality, water-based clear varnish so it doesn't yellow over time. Apply two coats, and this will protect your wood from splashes.
- You can add handles or knobs to the sides of your shelf so it's easier to pick up.
- Once all your paint and varnish has dried, it's time to run the bath! You've earned it. Pick your fave treats, grab a book and enjoy your soak.

Chapter Two

A Stitch in Time

A few years ago, I went to local sewing classes because I wanted to learn how to make cushions for my house, and once I had the hang of it, I was obsessed. You can do so many lovely things with fabric. There are lots of sewing projects and resources online, but I always tell people to start with the basics first, and then you won't feel overwhelmed when you dive a bit deeper.

Sewing does not have to be expensive either. I still use my bargain sewing machine, which I bought myself for a birthday treat. I think I got a spare change from a hundred euro down the middle aisle of the supermarket.

It's a great skill and loads of fun, but sewing is also practical. Whether you want to upcycle old clothes or create custom home decor pieces, having some sewing knowledge will help you along the way.

Sewing Essentials

I am a believer in buying what you need as you need it. As with all crafts, there are plenty of fancy gadgets and tools out there, but here are the basic sewing tools you need to get started.

Scissors

Fabric scissors
Pinking shears
General use scissors (for cutting paper)

Pins and Needles

Sewing pins
Pincushion
Seam ripper
Universal machine needles ★

Machine Tools

Spare bobbins
Gütermann thread
Iron and ironing board
Seam guide
Zipper foot

Measuring

Measuring tape
Clear ruler
A fabric pen
Sewing pattern paper

Iron and ironing board
Sewing machine

★ *The size of your needle depends on the thickness of your fabric.*
Lighter fabrics require smaller sewing needles, and heavier fabrics require larger sewing needles.

Sewing Machine Guide

There are many brands and models of sewing machine on the market, with all sorts of different features, so picking the right one can be tricky. You don't want to spend loads of money on a machine that will gather dust in its box. Here are my tips for finding the perfect one.

Second-Hand

If you are a sewing newbie and want a bargain, I would encourage you to shop second-hand or borrow a machine at first. You'll find some great bargains on second-hand websites, buy and sell pages, and your local social media. If you go down this route:

- Look for machines marked as 'new', 'barely used', 'unwanted present', etc.
- Where possible, ask the seller to demonstrate that the settings work on the machine.
- Check the manual to see if any bits are missing. Check for spare bobbins, the foot pedal, etc.
- Turn on the machine, check that the light works, then open the bobbin case and look for any build-up of fluff or dirt.
- It is always a good idea to get a second-hand machine serviced, so factor in this cost when considering the price.
- Once purchased, change the machine's needle for health and safety and hygiene reasons.

Vintage sewing machines are virtually indestructible, but they are harder to use, especially for beginners. They are also heavier and less practical. I have a vintage treadle machine, but I don't use it for everyday sewing. So, as pretty as vintage sewing machines are, if you are a beginner, I would avoid them.

Features

When looking for a sewing machine, you need to ask yourself: what do I want to make, and what do I need? If you are a beginner or only sew occasionally, then a basic electronic model will do the job. You should be able to pick one up for under €200. It is tempting to purchase a fancy, computerised machine with loads of stitch options, but if you plan to sew only smaller projects, then you may not need them. I use a basic Singer model that I purchased from a supermarket. They are generally around the €100 mark, and you'll see them on the shelves every few months.

If you plan on doing lots of dressmaking and crafting, then you can move into the mid-range sewing machines, which go from about €300 to €700. Look for ones that have lots of stitch options and an overlocking stitch; also those that come with a zipper foot, blind hem foot, narrow hem foot, and a piping foot, as these are handy for dressmaking and making items for your home. You can also get machines that come with embroidery attachments.

I remember attending a sewing convention a few years ago, and I was shocked when I saw machines running into the thousands of euro. If sewing is your business then you need to invest, but for everyday projects, don't get too caught up in the machine itself – you can always upgrade in years to come and pass your basic model on to a new crafter.

Envelope Cushion

One of the very first projects I learned to sew was an envelope cushion. I remember how excited I felt as I showed everyone this lovely thing I had made. I had the creative buzz, and I want you to get that same feeling! The envelope cushion is a perfect project for beginners, so gather your tools and let's get creating.

What you need

Tape measure, paper, pencil and scissors for template
1 metre of cotton fabric
Iron and ironing board
Fabric scissors
Pins
Sewing machine
Thread to match your fabric
A cushion pad

- I find it easiest to work from a template or pattern, and you can reuse it whenever you want to make more cushions. It also helps if you are making a few at a time.

- Using your tape measure and some paper, measure out your templates. You will have a front and a back template for this project. I made a 16 x 16 in (40 x 40 cm) cushion; allowing for a one-inch seam, I measured out 17 x 17 in (43 x 43 cm) on my paper. If you want to make a bigger or smaller cushion, then adjust your measurements, making sure to allow for a 1-in (2.5-cm) seam. For the back template, I measured out 17 x 14 in (43 x 35.5 cm). (We will use two back pieces and overlap them to make an 'envelope'.)

- Iron your fabric before cutting it; using crease-free fabric will give you a perfect cut. Pin your template to your fabric and cut using your fabric scissors. Cut one front piece and two back pieces. Cutting fabric is just as important as sewing your piece, so take your time. You want to cut the fabric as straight as possible.

See p185 for a brief explanation of the sewing terms you'll come across in this chapter.

- Next, you'll need to sew a 1-in hem on each of your back pieces, which will stop the fabric from fraying at the back opening. Make sure that you're hemming the longer (17-in) side of the back piece. Fold over half an inch and press it with your iron. Then fold it over itself another half an inch and press. Secure the hem with some sewing pins, then sew a straight stitch down the hem of your fabric. Start and end with a backstitch to secure your stitch and stop it from coming loose.

- You are now going to sew the three pieces together and form your cushion. The most important thing is to make sure you face the right (patterned) sides of your fabric together; remember that you are sewing with the cushion inside out. Place the front piece down with the right side facing you. Lay one of the back pieces on top with the wrong side facing you (so the right sides are now facing each other). The top of the back piece should be aligned with the top of the front piece, with the hem below. Add the other back piece, aligning the bottom with the bottom of the front piece; the hem should be above. Use plenty of pins to make sure the fabric stays in place when you are sewing.

- Take your material to the machine to sew. Make sure to leave your 1-in seam allowance; use the guide on the plate of your sewing machine. Start and end with a backstitch to stop your thread from unravelling. Sew all around the cushions.

- Once finished, remove the pins. Snip the corners to get rid of excess material before turning it right side out. Snipping the corners will also give you a nice pointed corner when you turn your cushion cover.

- My favourite part of a sewing project is turning it from inside out to right-side out – I get the crafter's buzz! Once you turn your fabric over, give it an iron to flatten the seams. Then add your cushion pad and have fun admiring and styling your lovely new cushion.

Super-Quick Scrunchie

You might remember having a wrist full of scrunchies back in the 1990s, or maybe that was just me! Well, the scrunchie is truly back in fashion, and for a sewing enthusiast, it's a great way to use up scrap fabric.

Like most of the projects in this book, you can take my measurements and tweak them to your liking. By expanding the width and length of the fabric, you can make an extra sassy chunky scrunchie. Cotton and poly-cotton fabrics are the easiest to use, as they don't have much stretch, but you can also use silk to create dainty silk scrunchies. If you use silk or satin, try to use clips instead of pins to avoid marking the material.

What you need

Fabric of your choice
Ruler and fabric marker
Fabric scissors
Elastic
Sewing pins
Sewing machine
Thread
A safety pin

- Measure and cut a piece of fabric. As a guide, mine was 22 in (56 cm) long and 3.5 in (9 cm) wide. My piece of elastic was 6 in (15 cm) long. I have a smaller wrist, so you can measure the elastic around your wrist and adjust the length to fit.

- Fold the fabric over lengthwise, with the right sides facing each other, and pin. Take this to the machine and do a straight stitch down the side of the material. You will have created a little tunnel.

- To help turn the fabric the right way out, use a safety pin and pin it to the bottom of the fabric. Pull the safety pin through the tunnel, and the material will be the right way out.

- Next, pin the safety pin to the tip of the elastic, then thread it through the tunnel. You will notice the fabric start to scrunch up. Tie a double knot in the elastic to secure it in place.

- Now we are going to sew up the scrunchie. Fold the two raw edges in on themselves. Pin them together and do a straight stitch on the machine to close the opening. You can also do a hand whip stitch to close the scrunchie if you prefer.

- Once you make one or two scrunchies, you will be flying. These take around twenty minutes to make, but you can make a batch at a time and give them to your pals as presents.

Reusable Makeup Pads

To try and be more sustainable when it comes to my beauty routine, I swapped single-use cotton pads for reusable ones. It's a good way to recycle old towels and use up fabric scraps, and you will save money by striking cotton pads off your shopping list. You can easily create a batch of these in whatever size suits you, and you just pop them in the washing machine (in a mesh laundry bag, if you have one) whenever they need a clean.

What you need

Tape measure, paper, pencil and scissors for template
Fabric scissors
Fabric marker
Old towels
Cotton or poly-cotton fabric
Pins
Sewing machine
Thread

- I make my circular makeup pads slightly larger than the ones you get in the shops, as I like a nice wide pad when cleansing my skin. To create a circular template, you can trace around the base of a tin can or a cup, depending on the size you would like. Allow ¼ inch (☐ cm) for your seam.
- Using your fabric scissors, cut one piece of towel fabric and one piece of cotton fabric.
- Place the right sides of the fabric together and pin. Stitch around the circle but leave a gap large enough to pull the fabric through. Remember to backstitch at the beginning and end of your stitching to prevent it from unravelling.
- Before pulling the fabric through, you can clip the curves, as this will give it more of a circular shape when you pull the fabric the right way.
- Using the gap, pull the fabric through so that the right side of the material is facing outwards.
- To close the opening, tuck the raw seams in and topstitch around the circular pad.
- These make great presents, particularly as stocking fillers or in gift baskets!

Reusable Dish Scrubbers

Washing the dishes isn't the most glamorous of jobs, but you can make it look prettier with your very own reusable cleaning sponges. These are quick to make and another great way to recycle old material. We're going to use an old fruit bag as filling. Do you know the ones that come with your oranges? Well, they make a nice scrubby, spongey centre, and it's one less thing for the waste bin!

What you need

Tape measure, paper, pencil and scissors for template
Old towels
Cotton or poly-cotton fabric
An old fruit bag or other filling
Fabric marker and ruler
Fabric scissors
Pins
Sewing machine
Thread

- As a guide, here are the measurements I used for my template: I cut a rectangle that measures 5.5 x 3.5 in (14 x 9 cm), and this includes a ½ in (1¼ cm) seam allowance.
- Before cutting your fabric, make sure to iron out any wrinkles. Use your fabric marker and a ruler to mark out your measurements. Cut one piece of your cotton material. Cut one piece of towel material. Cut three or four rectangles of netting. You can use more or less netting, depending on the thickness you want for your sponge.
- Now you sandwich the materials together. Place the netting down first, then lay the towel material on top of the netting, with the right side facing up. Lay the cotton fabric on top of the towel material, with the right sides facing each other. Pin the layers of material together.

I use my sponges for scrubbing the dishes, but if you use them in other areas of your home, remember that more powerful chemicals like bleach may stain the cotton material.

- Leave a large enough opening on one side. Stitch the four sides, but not the opening. Remember to backstitch at the beginning and end of your stitiching to prevent it from unravelling.
- Before turning the material, trim off any bulky excess fabric and clip the corners. Use the opening to gently turn the material, so the right side of the fabric is now facing outwards.
- You should have a sandwich with one side cotton, one side towel and the netting in the middle. You can poke out the corners if they are looking rounded.
- Fold the opening inwards and pin. Topstitch around the four sides of the sponge, as this will close the opening, but it also gives it a decorative topstitch.

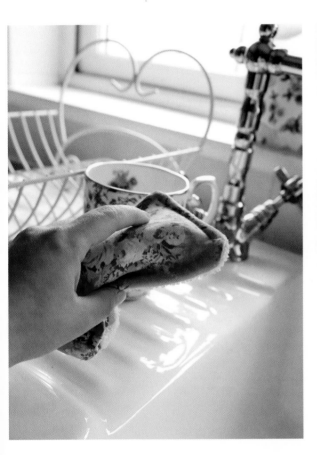

Pompom Cushion

A few years ago, I was in a high-end department store in London when I saw a cushion full of pompoms. I turned over the price tag and thought to myself, 'What? I could make that!' So I took the idea and tweaked it to make it my own. Pompoms are so fun – I remember making them in art class in primary school – but they do take a bit of time.

What you need

Wool in various colours
A pompom maker (or square of cardboard)
Fabric scissors
Envelope cushion (see page 44)
Needle and thread or fabric glue

- Let's begin with a little cheat: If you don't want to make an envelope cushion to stick the pompoms to, you can buy a cushion cover or use a second-hand one to save time.

- Begin by creating your pompoms. My envelope cushion is roughly 16 x 16 in (40 x 40 cm), and I made fifty pom poms.

- I use the old-school method to make my pompoms. (You can also buy a pompom maker.) Take a square of cardboard and cut a smaller square in the middle of it. Wind the wool around the piece of cardboard roughly one hundred times. Once wrapped, tightly tie a piece of wool around the middle of the wool. Cut the wool on either side and remove the pompom from the cardboard.

- You will notice that the pompom looks a little flat and floppy, so it's time to give it a haircut. Using sharp fabric scissors, trim the wool into more of a ball shape which should look thick and full.

- To stick the pompoms to the front of your envelope cushion, you have two options: a needle and thread to stitch each one on, or fabric glue. If using fabric glue, slide a piece of cardboard inside the cushion cover to stop the glue from sticking your front and back panels together. Follow the drying-time instructions on the back of your fabric glue.

- Have fun tweaking this to make it your own. You can make a smaller or larger cushion by adjusting the dimensions and using fewer or more pompoms; you can use different wools; or you can arrange the pompoms in different shapes and designs.

It's best to hand-wash the cushion and treat it gently as the pompoms can be delicate.

Fabric Clothes Hangers

A great way to practise making pockets and perfecting your topstitch is with these fabric clothes hanger covers. They pretty up your old plastic hangers, and if you have a dress you love, why not hang it up and display it on one of these? The added pocket also comes in handy for storing accessories that match your outfit. For beginners, I recommend using cotton or poly-cotton fabric. However, if you want to work with trickier fabric, you could use a silk or satin.

What you need

Tape measure, paper, pencil and scissors for template
Cotton or poly-cotton fabric
A hanger
Pins
Fabric marker
Fabric scissors
Thread
Sewing machine
An iron

- To create a template, use a pencil and paper and trace around the shape of your hanger. Once you get the rough shape of the hanger, you can add extra inches to the length, depending on how long you want your cover to be. Allow for an opening at the top for the hanger to go through. Add a ¼ inch (6 mm) seam allowance.
- Pin your template to your fabric and cut two pieces.

- For the pocket, cut a rectangular piece of fabric. Remember to cut slightly wider and longer than you need, to allow for the hem.
- Let's work on the pocket first. Hem the top of the rectangular piece of fabric by folding the material over and fold again to tuck the raw edge in, then do a straight stitch. Fold the remaining three sides of the fabric and iron the hem flat.
- Take one piece of your fabric, right side up, and pin your pocket in the centre. Topstitch the three sides of the pocket and remember to backstitch at the beginning and end of your stitiching to prevent it from unravelling.
- On the two pieces of fabric, hem the opening at the top that the hanger will go through.
- Place the right sides of the two pieces of fabric together and pin. Stitch the two 'arms', making sure not to stitch over the hemmed opening at the top or the raw-edge opening at the bottom.
- Pull the fabric the right way out and use your iron to fold over the raw edge at the bottom. Stitch a hem around this edge, which will be the opening you pull your clothes through.
- Once my project is complete, I like to iron it one more time to give it that professional finish. You can also use a zig-zag stitch, French seam or pinking shears to finish the raw edge of the fabric on the inside.

Beautiful Bunting

When I signed up for sewing classes, bunting was high on the list of items I was excited to make! I loved the idea of having floral bunting in my cottage kitchen. It's timeless: you can use it for parties and celebrations or leave it hanging in a sheltered spot in your garden. It adds fun to your space, and I always smile when I see it.

I try to avoid plastic or paper bunting from the shops; it just doesn't last as long. You can recycle old material or use your favourite patterned fabric for this project. Cotton and poly-cotton are best as they are easy to wash, so you can reuse them year after year.

What you need

Tape measure, paper, pencil and scissors for template
Cotton or poly-cotton fabric
Rotary tool, ruler and cutting mat (optional)
Fabric scissors
Fabric marker
Pins
Thread
Sewing machine
An iron
Bias binding (1½–2 metres)

- Create a triangle template for your bunting, using a piece of cardboard or paper. The sides of my triangles measured 9 in (23 cm) and the base was 6 in (16 cm).

- Pin your template to your fabric and cut out the triangles. When cutting out multiple pieces of fabric, I find a rotary tool, ruler and cutting mat handy; but if you don't have these, a fabric scissors and template will do the job. Cut two pieces of fabric per flag, so if you want nine flags, you need eighteen triangles.

- Place two triangles together, with the right sides of the material facing each other. Pin the fabric and straight stitch the two long sides of the triangle. Leave the bottom open. A ½ in (1¼ cm) seam allowance is perfect for your flags.

- Snip the excess fabric on the tip of the triangle, as this will give you a pointed corner when you turn it the right side out. Iron your flags flat, and gently poke out the corner of the triangle if yours is rounded. Trim off any excess material.

- When you have all your flags stitched, it's time to place them on your bias binding. You can make your own bias binding, but for a project like this, shop-bought is fine. Your bias binding will be one long strip. Fold the length in half and iron, as this will give you a flap for the flags to go in.

- Place your flags on the bias binding, with an equal distance between each flag. Lift the bias and place each flag inside the flap, then securely pin.

- Straight stitch the length of the bias, and as you sew over each flag, they will be secured. Trim off any loose threads (or whiskers, as I like to call them!), and you've just made your very own fabric bunting.

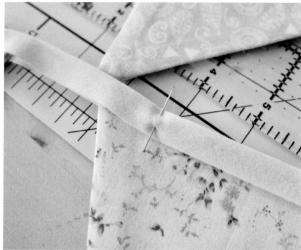

Memory Cushion

I love to make memory cushions and bears for people, taking their loved one's clothing and stitching it into sentimental keepsakes. When I was twenty, I lost my father, so I know all too well the pain of grief and loss, and I know how a piece of clothing can bring back memories and give comfort in times of sorrow. With a memory cushion, it feels like a part of that person lives in your home, and unlike a photo, it can be squeezed, hugged and held. I know it's scary to consider cutting clothes of sentimental value, but here are my tips for transforming them into a memory cushion.

Picking the perfect fabric

Try to find clothes made from cotton and poly-cotton, which don't stretch too much. Men's shirts and jeans and women's dresses and skirts work well and have lots of material in them. You can also mix different pieces of clothing to create a unique cushion. For beginners, avoid knitwear, silks and material that is stretchy. To build your confidence, practise on old items of your own or clothes from a second-hand shop.

What you need

Tape measure, paper, pencil and scissors for template
Old items of clothing
Pins
Fabric scissors
Fabric marker
An iron
Thread
Sewing machine
A cushion pad

- Begin by creating a template. I drew out 17 x 17 in (43 x 43 cm) square on some paper for the front of the cushion, and a 17 x 14 in (43 x 35.5 cm) piece for the back. These measurements include a 1-inch seam allowance that will make a 16-inch cushion.
- Iron your fabric, then pin on the template and cut one piece of material for the front and two pieces for the back.

- If you use a shirt, do a line of stitching down the middle to stop the buttons from gaping open when you add your cushion pad.
- Sew a 1-in (2.5 cm) hem onto one of the long sides of your back piece. Using your iron, fold over half an inch and press, then fold it over again and press. Secure with some pins and do a straight top-stitch. Do this for both back pieces.
- You are now going to sew the three pieces together. Place the front piece down with the patterned side of the fabric facing up. Lay a back piece of fabric on top, making sure the two right sides of the material face each other. Line up the sides and corner, and then add the third piece before pinning the fabric together.
- Allow for a 1-in (2.5 cm) seam allowance. Sew all around your cushion and use a backstitch to keep your stitches in place.
- Once your cushion is sewn, you can clip the corners and turn it right side out. Iron it again before inserting a cushion pad.
- You're now ready to give this lovely gift, or to keep it for yourself as a memory of someone special.

Sparkly Christmas Stockings

There is a certain magic in the air around Christmas time. I love the twinkly lights and sitting by the fire, all toasty and cosy. And I love decorating for Christmas – it's so much fun to change your home decor completely for a few weeks of the year. To add a little extra sparkle to my mantle, I created these sequin Christmas stockings. They're easy to make, and you can customise them to any size and shape you want.

What you need

Tape measure, paper, pencil and scissors for template
Old Christmas stocking (optional)
Sequin material
Fabric scissors
Fusible interfacing
An iron
Pins
Thread
Sewing machine
Faux fur trim
Ribbon

- To create your template, trace around an old Christmas stocking and add an extra ½ inch (1¼ cm) for the seam allowance. If you don't have an old stocking, use a plate to trace the curve and a ruler for the straight bits.
- Pin your template to your material. Cut two pieces of sequin material and two pieces of fusible interfacing, which will give your stocking structure and stop it from flopping. Apply the fusible interfacing to the wrong side of your material and iron it, following the heat instructions.
- Place the two stocking pieces together with the right sides facing each other and pin. Straight stitch around the sides and leave the top open.
- Now let's work on the faux fur trim. This trim will be a fold-over collar, which can be tricky. If you are a beginner, you could skip this step, hem the raw edge instead and add a ribbon to hang your stocking. Measure the faux fur trim so that it is the same width as the opening. Pin the trim with the right side of the fur to the wrong side of the stocking, matching the seams.

- Sandwich the ribbon between the sequin material and the trim.
- Straight stitch around the opening of the stocking to secure the trim to the stocking.
- Clip the corners before turning the stocking the right way out. When you turn your stocking, the wrong side of the trim will be facing. Fold over the collar to reveal the faux fur trim.
- Add some bows or embellishments to bling up your stockings before placing them in your favourite spot.

Safety first! Don't place stockings or decorations near an open fire or a stove that is in use.

Easter Bunnies

These adorable bunnies will add a touch of cuteness to your Easter tablescape. You could also use them to create bunny bunting! They are quick to make and can be sewn by hand; just follow the steps below and hand-sew instead of using a sewing machine.

What you need

Tape measure, paper, pencil and scissors for template
Cotton or poly-cotton fabric
Pins
Fabric scissors
Fabric marker
Felt
Thread
Sewing machine (optional)
Pinking shears
Stuffing

- To create your template, draw out two circles, a smaller head one above and a larger belly one below. Add two small half-circles to the corners of the belly as the feet. Then draw bunny ears at the top of the head circle. It's best not to make your bunny too small, as it may be harder to add the stuffing later.
- Pin the template to your material and carefully cut it with your fabric scissors. Cut one piece of material for the front of the bunny.
- Pin the bunny material to a piece of felt. Stitch around the bunny shape to secure it to the felt, leaving a small opening on the side of the belly for the filler. Remember to backstitch at the beginning and end of your stitiching to prevent it from unravelling.

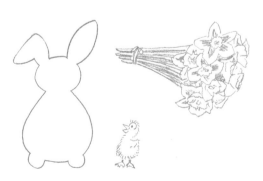

- Take pinking shears and cut around the bunny shape. Some pinking shears give a zigzag cut, but the ones I used (which you can buy online) left a scalloped edge.
- Carefully add your filler to stuff the bunny. You can purchase soft toy filler in most craft shops, but cushion or pillow filler is fine. You don't need to use a lot.
- Close the opening with a hand stitch or your machine. For extra cuteness, tie a ribbon around the bunny's neck. If you are using these on your Easter table, you could add name tags for your guests.

To make bunny bunting, create a batch of bunnies by following the steps above (stuffing optional). Use thick string for a rustic look or sew them to bias binding, as on page 62.

Easy-Sew Kids Apron

When I first started sewing, I always bought patterns to work from. These can be costly, so as I became more experienced, I began using old clothes as a template instead. Not only as a money-saver, but it's also a great way to build your confidence and your sewing skillset.

To make this apron, I used one of my niece's dungaree dresses as a guide. I knew the dress fit her, so it was a perfect base for my project. If you'd like an apron for yourself, you can use a garment from your wardrobe as a template.

What you need

Tape measure, paper, pencil and scissors for template
Cotton or poly-cotton fabric
Fabric marker
Fabric scissors
Pins
An iron
Thread
Sewing machine

- To create a template, I traced around the front of my niece's dress and added an inch to allow for the seam. This template can be used for making larger aprons too – just add extra inches to the sides and length. Before cutting, it's a good idea to hold the template up to the person you're making it for, just to check that it's wide and long enough.
- Use fabric scissors to cut out your apron. I used drop-cloth fabric here, which is very practical and machine-washable, but it can fray easily, so I took my time at this stage.
- For the straps, I measured the width of those on my niece's dress. In terms of length, I judged myself what would be long enough to fit around to the back of her waist and neck; you could also measure

the person to find the right length. Add an extra two to three inches to allow for tying a knot.

- For the strap template, double these measurements. Trace this onto your material and cut out four pieces, two for the neck ties and two for the waist ties.
- Fold the length of the strap fabric in half and iron, then fold again into quarters and iron. Use pins to secure the strap in place. Topstitch two straight stitches down the length of your strap.
- Next, pin the neck straps and waist straps where you want them, making sure each pair is symmetrical.
- Then it's time to hem around the apron. Using your iron, fold up once, then fold again and press. You can add pins to secure your hems before sewing on the machine. Take your time when sewing your topstitch, and backstitch over the straps to make them more secure.
- A pocket can come in very handy for little artists (see page 58 for more photos of making a pocket). To add one to your apron, measure the front and decide how big you want the pocket to be. Add a ½ in (1¼ cm) seam allowance to your measurements.
- Cut a rectangular piece of fabric with your measurements. Hem the top of the rectangular piece of fabric by folding the material over and folding again to tuck the raw edge in, then do a straight stitch.
- Fold in and iron the remaining three sides of the fabric.
- Pin the picket to the centre of the apron fabric. Topstitch the three sides of the pocket and remember to do a backstitch at the beginning and end of your stitch.
- Finally, iron your new apron to give it a professional finish.

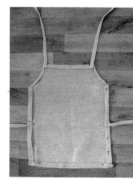

If your apron is for a child, you might want to use Velcro on the straps instead. Use your judgment – the great thing about this project is that it's completely customisable.

Pencil Case

Making a pencil case or a zipped pouch is a fun way to practise sewing zips. When I was learning to sew, I had an unfortunate incident with a zip that knocked my confidence! My lining got caught, and instead of unpicking it and trying again, I threw the whole thing in the bin. The sewing rage gets us all from time to time, but the magic really is in the mistakes! So don't be afraid or disheartened – if you mess up, unpick that thread and try again.

Below, I offer two measurements for this project; the larger one is perfect as a makeup bag.

What you need

Tape measure, paper, pencil and scissors for template
Two types of cotton or poly-cotton fabric, one patterned and one plain
Lightweight woven fusible interfacing
Pins
Fabric scissors
Iron
A zip
Thread
Pinking shears
Sewing pins
Sewing machine zipper foot
Ribbon or string for a side pull (optional)

- Measure and cut out a paper template. Here are two suggested sizes:

    Smaller pencil case: 10 in (26 cm) wide, 5 in (13 cm) long and use a 10-in (26 cm) zip.

    Larger pencil case: 14 in (35.5 cm) wide, 9 in (23 cm) long and use a 14-in (35.5 cm) zip.

    For the pull tabs, cut two pieces of ribbon 2½ in (6□ cm) long.

- Pin your template to the fabrics and cut to size. You will need one piece of the patterned fabric for the body (outer piece), one piece of the plain fabric for the lining, and one piece of lightweight woven fusible interfacing.

- Using an iron, fuse the interfacing to the wrong side of the patterned piece of fabric, following the heat instructions. The interfacing will give your pencil case structure.

- Next, we'll tackle the zip. Lay your patterned piece of fabric on your table with the right side facing up. Lay your zip face down on the patterned piece of fabric, lining the zipper tape to the edge of the

material. Lay the lining piece of fabric on top, lining up the edges. The two pieces of fabric should be right sides together. Use clamps or pins to keep it all in place.

- Using a zipper foot on your sewing machine, stitch at ¼ in (☐ cm) seam allowance with a straight stitch. Remember to backstitch.

- When the zipper pull gets in the way of the presser foot, you might be tempted to try and stitch past it, but you will get a wobbly line of stitching. To keep your stitches straight, sew halfway down the zip, leave the needle in the fabric, and lift the presser foot. Then, zip the zipper pull past the presser foot up to the area you've already sewn. Lower the foot and finish the seam.

- Using your iron, press the material. When you lay your fabric down, the zip will be facing upwards.

- With your zip right side up, fold the outer fabric so that the opposite long edge is right side down on top of the zip. Flip the pouch over, so that the zip is now the wrong side up, and fold the lining fabric so that the opposite long edge is also right side down on top of the zip. Pin or clip in place and stitch.

- You will now have a tube or roll of inside-out fabric! Pull one end of the tube through from the other end so that the right side of the patterned fabric is on the outside of the tube. Unzip your zip to give yourself a bit of room to manoeuvre.

- Then, give the tube a good press with your iron and topstitch close to the edge of the zip on both sides of the outer fabric. The topstitching on either side of your zip can be a bit fiddly, but it's definitely worth the effort as it gives your pencil case a really nice, tidy finish.

- The hardest part is done! Turn the tube inside out again – the lining will be on the outside – and we will work on closing the side seams and boxing the corners.

- You can now trim the excess material from your zip. When shortening a zip, use regular scissors to cut the teeth, as it will damage your fabric scissors.

- Flatten your pencil case so that the zip is in the middle. Insert the material you want to use as pull tabs into the two sides. You want the looped end of the tab inside the pouch, with the raw edges of the tab lined up with the raw edges of the pouch.

- Straight stitch the two sides.

- Now we will box off all four corners. Pinch the corner fabric out into a triangle shape and use your ruler and fabric marker to draw a line over the corner. Make sure to measure in the same length on each corner.

- Stitch across all four corners and use your pinking shears to cut off the excess. If you don't have pinking shears, you could also trim the excess with fabric scissors and then do a zigzag stitch. Turn the pencil case the right way out and poke the corners in, and you now have a boxy shape pencil case!

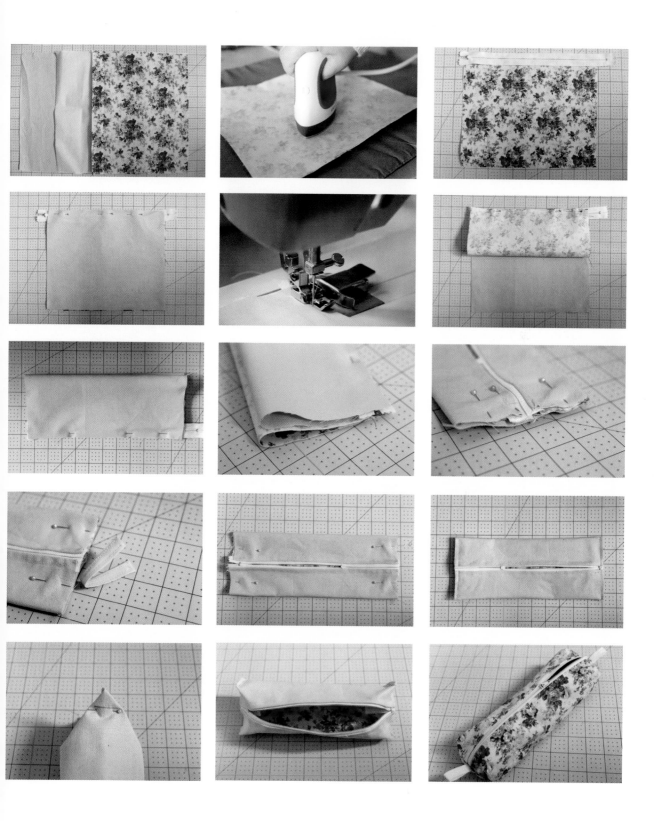

Chapter Three

Reuse and Refresh, Small

Whether it is an empty milk carton or a discarded bike wheel, an old gin bottle or a piece of furniture in need of some love, nothing gives me more pleasure than taking something unwanted and making it sing again.

Sustainability is a hot topic, and rightly so. We need to mind our planet, to reuse and recycle as much as we can. I am not perfect on this front, but every small step adds up. In the next two sections of the book, I will share some upcycling projects – for small items as well as big – to help you think in a new way about old things.

Children use their imaginations and see a shoebox as a dollhouse and a tin can as a phone – even a toilet roll has endless possibilities! As we get older, we lose the ability to see things differently, to break away from the usual. To be creative, we need to start thinking like a child again!

Remember back when you were a kid, if you were bored, you'd be told to go outside and play. Quickly, a stick would become a bow and arrow, and a tree would become a fort. Nowadays, we self-soothe with technology; we cram our free time with tasks and are addicted to being busy. (I am certainly guilty of this!) Let yourself be bored for an hour, without distractions, and see what fresh ideas come into your mind.

Milk Carton Baskets

We'll start with an easy project: turning an empty milk carton into a mini basket, which is perfect for storing stationery on your desk or cosmetics in your bathroom. Put your own stamp on it by getting creative with colours and fabrics.

What you need (for the basket)

Milk carton
Craft knife or scissors
Glue gun or craft glue
Lollipop sticks
Acrylic paint
Twine or ribbon (optional)

What you need (for the lining)

Ruler and fabric marker or pencil
Cotton fabric
Fabric scissors
Sewing pins
Thread
Sewing machine (or needle for hand stitching)
Iron

- Before you begin, make sure to clean your milk carton thoroughly with warm, soapy water.
- Measure your carton, mark the height you want, and cut the top off evenly all the way around using a sharp craft knife or scissors.
- Use your glue gun or craft glue to apply lollipop sticks to the outside of the carton. Apply a small bead of glue, then press your sticks firmly.
- I painted my lollipop sticks white, but you can leave the natural wood or use other colours. You could also stain the wood for a rustic effect. Apply one or two coats of acrylic paint to the wooden sticks and allow the paint to dry.

- To create the fabric liner, measure the base of the carton and the height and width of its walls. You can trace the measurements out on paper if it is easier. Add extra length to the fabric so you have enough material to roll over the lip of the carton. For mine, I cut four 6 x 3½ in (15 x 9 cm) rectangles of fabric for the sides and one 3 x 3 in (8 x 8 cm) square for the base.

- Next, you essentially create a box shape but with fabric. Pin the patterned (right) sides of the four 'walls' together and stitch the four seams. Then pin the base to the sides and stitch it. Remember, patterned sides of fabric facing each other.

- Once the base is stitched on, sew a hem onto the lip at the top. Use your iron to get a neat finish. Insert your fabric liner into the basket and fold over the fabric on top. Add some twine or a ribbon, then figure out what you're going to store in your lovely new mini basket!

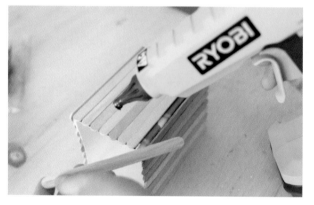

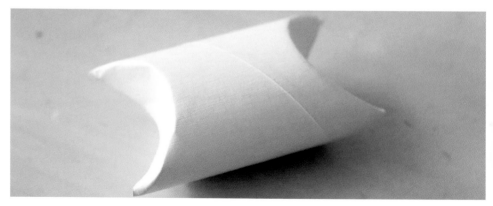

TP Treasure Boxes

As every kid knows, empty toilet rolls have many uses! Did you know they make great seedling pots for your garden? Here, we'll transform them into pretty gift boxes, which are particularly nice as stocking stuffers or wedding favours.

If you are worried about hygiene, I understand. Before you start out, pour some distilled water and vinegar into a spray bottle, add a few drops of lemon or tea tree essential oil and shake. Spritz the cardboard and allow it to dry. These essential oils have antibacterial properties and leave the rolls smelling amazing too.

What you need

Empty toilet rolls
Acrylic paint and brush
Decorative napkins
PVA or découpage glue
Clear varnish (optional)
Ribbon or twine

- Fold the sides of each toilet roll inwards to create a flap for opening and closing.
- Using your paintbrush, apply two coats of acrylic paint and allow this to fully dry. This will make a nice backdrop for the découpage.
- Gently tear the decorative pattern from your napkin. Peel the layers until it is at its thinnest ply. Apply a little découpage glue or PVA glue to the cardboard and gently place the napkin on top. Use your brush to smooth out the wrinkles. Apply another layer of glue over the napkin and allow it to dry.
- You can apply a layer of clear varnish to the toilet roll to seal in your découpage and protect it from dirt. This is optional, as PVA glue will dry hard and offer a small amount of protection.
- Once you are happy with your tiny boxes, pop in an item of your choice and fold over. Decorate with some pretty ribbon or twine and add a gift tag too.

Tin Can Candles

Have a rummage in the recycling bin, and you will usually find some old tin cans. There are endless ways to upcycle tins – use them as vases or plant pots, bird feeders, wind chimes, even for baking bread! – and here, I will share how to turn them into scented candles. I used fabric scraps on the outsides, but you can use techniques from previous chapters to paint and decorate them too.

What you need

Tins cans

Sandpaper

Saucepan

Heat-resistant bowl ★

Candle wax

Essential oils

Candle wicks

Candle-making thermometer

Glue gun

Scrap fabric to decorate

★ *Not to be reused for cooking*

- For this project, I used soy wax and wood wicks. See page 24 for info on the other kinds of wax you can use. Before you start, leave your tin cans to steep in warm, soapy water for a while. The labels will fall off, and then you can give the outsides a good clean. The edges of metal cans can be sharp; to avoid any unwanted cuts, use some sandpaper to soften the sharp edges.

- Create a double boiler by heating water in a saucepan and adding a bowl on top. Add your wax flakes to the bowl. I melted 1 lb (454 g) of wax, which was enough for two large candles, but you can double up if you'd like a bigger batch or split it into three smaller candles.

- Once the wax has melted, take it off the heat and add your scent. I added one tablespoon (15 ml) of essential oils per large candle – two tablespoons (30 ml) for the whole 1 lb batch – which is quite light. It was summer when I made mine, so I used a blend of citronella and peppermint. When it comes to adding your essential oil to wax, the optimum temperature is between 85°C and 93°C (185°F and 200°F) depending on what wax you melt. Use a candle thermometer to check the temperature.

- Add wicks to the base of the tin cans, securing them with a dollop of glue. If you use cotton wicks, you can use a chopstick or spoon to hold them in place as you pour. Very carefully, pour the wax into the tins and allow them time to set.

- Once your candles have hardened, it's time to decorate. I cut scrap fabric pieces that were slightly larger than the cans, and I ironed over the raw edges on all sides of the fabric. I used my glue gun to stick the fabric to the cans and added some string around the middle for decoration.

- Instead of fabric, you could paint your tins with some chalk or acrylic paint and use a stencil to add design. I always say, take the idea and make it your own!

Bicycle Wheel Wall Art

I remember the day I found this old bike wheel. I was out walking when I saw it discarded in some bushes. It was still bright out, and I was too embarrassed to walk all the way home carrying it, so the next day I got up early and drove back over!

I decided to create a floral wreath using the wheel as my base. Floristry isn't a skill of mine, but I do adore floral displays and experimenting with fresh and faux flowers.

You might not be so lucky as to find a wheel at the side of the road, but you can look in salvage yards and on second-hand websites. You could also reach out to a bike-repair shop and ask if they have any bent or broken wheels – just make sure to check for rust and rot.

What you need

Degreaser
Steel wool
Spray paint primer
Spray paint
Safety gloves
Faux flowers
Pliers
Florist wire

- Before applying primer and paint, give your wheel a deep clean. Using a degreaser and steel wool, scrub the wheel to remove as much grime as you can.

- Apply one coat of primer to the wheel; I used a grey colour. It might be tempting to skip this step, but primer helps the spray paint adhere to the metal and prevents peeling.

- When your primer is dry, apply two coats of topcoat; I used a bright copper colour. You should find the drying time on the back of your can of spray paint. Once dry, you now have the perfect base for your floral wreath.

- Using a set of pliers, cut the wire stems off your faux flowers, leaving just a small amount of stem at the base. You might want to wear a gardening glove for this part. I like to arrange my flowers before attaching them; that way, I can move the flowers around to get the display I want. Get creative and mix foliage with the flower heads.

Attach a strap to the wheel if you want to hang it on a wall.
Make sure your hook is strong, as the wheel will have some weight.

• Use your florist wire to attach the flowers to the wheel. This is the fiddliest bit, so take your time. Trim off any excess wire, which can be sharp. You can also use a glue gun here, but florist wire is easier to remove if you want to change the style of your flower wreath in the future. Once all your flowers are attached, lift the wreath and check for loose flowers.

Fabric Zip Pouches

We all have items of clothing in our wardrobes that we hold on to in the hopes of fitting into them one day. Well, I certainly do! With the damage fast fashion does to the planet, I always try to find ways to reuse fabrics rather than buying new. Preloved clothes, curtains and bedsheets are all perfect for upcycling. Whether you turn them into a new piece of clothing or decor for your home, there are loads of ways to give them a new life.

Here, I will share how I turned an old dress into fabric pouches for me and my friends. This is a lovely way to reuse an old item of clothing, particularly one with an attractive fabric. If you're a newbie, choose items made from cotton or cotton-blend with no stretch, as they are easier to sew than silks and satin.

What you need

Tape measure, paper, pencil and scissors for template
Two types of cotton or poly-cotton fabric, one patterned and one plain
Lightweight woven fusible interfacing
Fabric scissors
Iron
An 8-in (20 cm) zip
Sewing pins
Thread
Sewing machine zipper foot

- Using a pencil and paper, trace out a pattern for your pouches. Mine measured 9 in (23 cm) wide, 6 in (15 cm) long, and 2 in (5 cm) to square off the corners. (You'll see the shape in the photo on the next page.) You can customise the dimensions to make a smaller or larger pouch.

- When I refer to the 'outer' piece in these instructions, I mean the exterior, patterned piece of fabric, which is cut from the old piece of clothing. To avoid confusion, I recommend using a different plain fabric for the lining of your pouch. The first step is to cut two pieces of patterned fabric and two pieces of plain using your template. Also cut two pieces of lightweight woven fusible interfacing.

- Using an iron, fuse the interfacing to the wrong side of the patterned pieces of fabric, following the heat instructions.

- Next, it's time to install the zip on the first side. On your desk, place one outer piece of fabric right side up, with the straight edge closest to you. Take your zip and place it right side down on top of that, with the zipper pull to the right, aligning the edge of the zipper tape with the straight edge of the

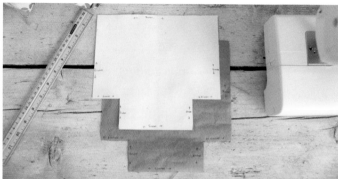

fabric. Finally, place one of the lining pieces on top, right side down. Use pins to secure your fabric sandwich together.

• Using a zipper foot on your sewing machine, stitch at ¼ inch (□ cm) seam allowance with a straight stitch. A zipper foot allows you to get closer to the zip as you sew, without the foot getting in the way.

• Place the second outer fabric piece right side up on your table. Place the zip right side down on top of it. The already-stitched first sandwich will be attached on the other side of the zipper tape, with the zipper pull on the left this time. Place the lining piece on top of the zip, right side down. Clamp your layers together and straight stitch the long edge.

• Now, lay your pouches out flat and iron the outer and lining pieces away from the zip, then topstitch close to the edge of the zip. A topstitch will give it a nice professional finish.

• Open your zip. This is an important step, as if you do not open your zip, you won't be able to pull your fabric through. Open out the layers of fabric and place so that the right sides of the outer fabric are facing each other. The right sides of the lining fabric will also end up facing each other. Pin.

• Sew from one edge of the outer piece, down each side, and along the bottom. Use the ½ inch (1¼ cm) seam allowance. Do not stitch the bottom corner openings. Stitch the sides and the bottom of the two lining pieces, making sure to leave an opening in the bottom seam for turning. Iron the side seams open.

• To box off the corners, pin the right sides of the fabric together and align the seams. Straight stitch across the corner to create the boxed corner. Trim away excess material. Do this on all four corners.

• Turn your pouch right side out, and this can be fiddly! Then poke out your corner and stitch the opening in the lining closed. Push the lining to the inside, and you are all done!

Vintage Plate Clock

When rummaging in the charity shops, I see lots of china, porcelain and patterned crockery. I'm a bit of a magpie, and I find it hard to walk past! Mismatched china can look beautiful when styled for a vintage tea party. And if you have a single plate, let me show you how to turn it into a clock. This project is more advanced, but don't be put off by the idea of drilling through china – if you don't fancy it, you can always ask for help with that part.

What you need

A vintage plate
Masking tape
Measuring tape and ruler
Safety goggles
A drill
An 8 mm tile and glass drill bit or diamond tip drill bit
A cup of water
A clock-making kit and a battery
A plate stand or wall hook (optional)

- When choosing a plate, keep in mind that the thinner it is, the easier it is to drill through. However, thin plates can also crack, so take your time when drilling. You might want to practise on an old piece of crockery before tackling your plate clock.
- Begin by placing two pieces of masking tape at the centre of the china plate in a cross shape. You will drill through the masking tape, which stops the china from cracking.
- Measure the plate to find the centre and mark it with a pen.
- Wearing your safety goggles, load your drill with an 8 mm tile drill bit and slowly drill a hole in the centre of the plate. Apply a small amount of pressure, but let the drill do the work. The key to drilling through ceramics or tile is to keep the drill bit cool and lubricated, so pause every few seconds and dip the tip of the drill bit into a cup of cold water.

- Next, assemble your clock kit. You can buy one cheaply online or in some craft stores, and it should come with detailed instructions – I found mine quite easy to put together. My tip is to be gentle with the clock hands, as they are delicate and bend easily. Once you pop in the battery, your clock should start working.

- You can add a hook to the back if you want to hang your clock on a wall, or use a plate stand to display it on a mantle, on a bookshelf or in the kitchen. Anywhere that you can show people and say, 'Look, I made this!'

Glass Bottle Vase

Another item that's in everyone's recycle bin is a glass bottle. Here, I'll share with you how to cut an empty bottle and transform it into a vase or a planter for your succulents. Cutting glass is doable, but it is more advanced than some of our other crafts, so ask for help if you're not feeling confident.

Liquor bottles are perfect for this project, with their lovely round shapes and pretty details within the glass. They transform beautifully into lamps and vases.

Get in some practice to master your technique before cutting your favourite bottle. Some bottles can crack, and some may already have cracks in the glass that you cannot see, which will cause them to shatter.

There are many ways to cut glass, from alcohol on a string to a candle flame, but you can pick up a bottle-cutting tool for around €20 online. This is the safest method to use and will help you to avoid messy mistakes or accidents.

What you need

Glass liquor bottle
Safety goggles
Heat-resistant safety gloves
A glass bottle cutter
Hot and cold water
Medium- and fine-grit sandpaper

- Before cutting the bottle, check for any visible cracks or damage. I suggest cutting your glass bottle next to a sink. Have a kettle of boiling water ready and the cold tap on standby. Wear safety goggles and gloves.
- Set up the bottle cutter and adjust it to fit. Firmly turn the bottle towards you to create a scoreline, and make sure to keep it as even as possible.
- Bring the bottle to the sink and slowly pour boiling water over the scoreline. Then run cold water from the tap over the scoreline. The bottle should separate, so be ready to catch any falling glass. If the bottle does not come apart on the first try, pour boiling water and then cold water over the scoreline again. For some large bottles with thicker glass, you may need to try a few times.
- Once the glass is cut, sand and smooth the rough edge. Start with medium-grit sandpaper and work your way up to fine-grit.

- You can use your cut bottle as a vase or a terrarium. If you would like to use it as a planter, add some drainage holes or use a specialist succulent soil. To cut holes in the glass base, follow the steps on page 99 where I share how to drill through ceramics – it's the same method for glass and tile.

- For newbies, it can be intimidating to play with new materials such as glass and tile, but I really hope you are inspired to try. 'Try and fail, but never fail to try.'

Chapter Four

Reuse and Refresh, Big

When I bought my first home, I wanted to fill it with pretty furniture, but there was very little money left in the pot. I remember being in an interiors workshop and the lovely owner suggested painting an old piece that I wasn't sure about – until that moment, it had never crossed my mind to upcycle furniture to put my own stamp on it and bring it back to life. From then on, no piece of second-hand furniture was safe! I took bits from my friends and family and scoured buy-and-sell websites and social media marketplaces for pieces to make over.

Most of my furniture upcycling projects involve painting, which might seem like an intimidating prospect to a beginner. Believe me, in my almost ten years at it, I've had all sorts of problems and made plenty of mistakes, from chippy paint to bleeding oils – but I've honed my skills, and now it's one of my favourite pastimes! In the age of disposable, cheap furniture, it feels good to reuse rather than replace.

In this chapter, I will give tips on how to find the best second-hand pieces and break down all the upcycling steps, from prepping and stripping to painting your furniture.

Second-Hand Treasure Hunt

Whether you're searching online, browsing the flea markets, or you just come across a full skip while out for a walk, nothing beats the buzz of finding second-hand goodies for your home. Here are my top tips for choosing preloved furniture. It can be tempting to grab as many free items as you can, especially in the beginning, but please learn from my mistakes or you will end up with a very full shed!

Where to look

Let's start with online. Nowadays, second-hand websites are popular and a great way to make money when you're having a clear-out. One man's junk is another man's treasure! Set specific alerts for the type of furniture or items you want, so you won't be tempted to buy loads of other things you do not need.

Social media platforms are another way to find local buy-and-sell groups or individuals selling or giving away items in your area. These can be more difficult to search, but you can get in touch and ask if they have a particular piece.

Friends and family! Now, this one comes with a warning. Maybe it is an Irish thing, but we love to give people stuff – stuff they might not always need! And we are too polite to say no, which can result in a shed full of chairs and other random bits and pieces (believe me!). When reaching out to your loved ones, be specific with what you want. If you need a table but your aunt is throwing out chairs, do not take them just because they're free.

Most of my furniture is second-hand and upcycled. The bed frame I sleep on cost just €50! I usually buy online, but you can also hunt in charity shops. Some charities even have dedicated furniture stores and warehouses, and it's nice knowing you're supporting a worthy cause.

We don't have massive flea markets here like in other parts of the world, but we have plenty of smaller markets all around the country. You won't generally find furniture at them – other than dedicated vintage-furniture fairs, which tend to be expensive – but you may find other small pieces to upcycle.

One of my favourite things about shopping second-hand is the community. Anytime I go to collect an item, I have great chats with the seller. You can ask them the history of the piece you're buying, and you might end up with something else cool. Once I went to buy a Royal Albert tea set and came home with a vintage phone, which is still sitting on my desk!

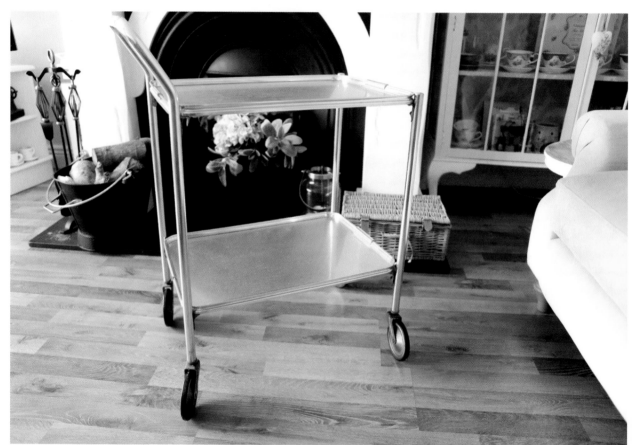

Be specific and set a budget

Just because an item is free does not mean you need it! I still battle with this one, but in recent times I've realised none of us need as much as we think we do. Homes fill up quickly, and you want a nice balanced space and not an overwhelmingly cluttered one.

Write yourself a list of what you need. If you need a chest of drawers, try to put your blinkers on and search only for that. Admire the pretty free stuff but leave it there. Be strict about measurements, too; buying furniture that is too large for your home is a common mistake.

Also, be patient! In a fast-fashion world, we want to have things *now* – but often you will find something that fits your home better if you wait.

Don't pay too much. Even if you end up in a bidding war online or a seller won't budge on price, stick to your budget. It's never worth getting yourself into debt by overstretching your purse. Another piece will come along, so just be patient and enjoy the hunt.

What to check for

It is a good idea to check second-hand furniture for damage, but don't let it put you off – if it's a broken piece of glass or a wobbly leg, you can pay to have it repaired or tackle it yourself. Just make sure to factor repairs into the cost. I tend to avoid items that have serious water damage or warping in the wood. A small amount of mould can be cleaned, but it could be a sign of wood rot and you don't want to bring that into your home.

Avoid woodworm! It is caused by wood-boring beetles that lay their eggs within exposed pieces of wood. One way to spot woodworm is to check for clusters of tiny, neat holes in the wood, which are created by woodworms on the way out after laying their eggs. If you see dust around the area, this means they may still be active. Also, the wood may crumble in your hand when touched. Woodworm can be treated and repaired, but if you are a beginner, I suggest avoiding these pieces. Woodworms are typically attracted to damp and wet surfaces, so make sure to check your shed or garage for damp before storing any items there.

Measure twice! It's very easy to buy items that are the wrong size. I am guilty of this, and I spent years manoeuvring around my second-hand sofa that was too wide for my small living room. Items tend to look smaller in pictures and shops. Measure it up and then bring the dimensions home to see how it will fit before buying. Can you easily move around it? Will it block a door? Can you open the door without it hitting something? How will it look against the other pieces in the room? Just a few of the questions to help you pick the perfect item for your space.

Upcycling Essentials

As with sewing, I think it's best to build your upcycling toolkit over time. Buy tools as you need them, and that way you can invest in good-quality and long-lasting materials. Still, there are some basics that are handy to have around. You can pick them up easily from hardware and craft shops.

Protection

Protective glasses
Gloves
Mask or respirator

Yes, we crafters were wearing masks before 2020! An N95 mask is best, as it filters out even the tiniest of particles. Cotton face masks will not keep out sawdust and other particles from upcycling.

Preparation

Sugar soap
Degreaser
Sanding blocks and sandpaper
Painter's tape
Tack cloths

Sugar soap and degreaser are for cleaning your items before upcycling. You can buy sugar soap in some budget shops, and you will find it in the hardware shop. It's always good to have sanding blocks and sheets in different grits to hand, as you will be lightly sanding furniture before painting. Tack cloths absorb dust, so they're great for wiping away dust after sanding. I also use old towels cut up into rags for cleaning.

Painting

Foam roller and tray
Paintbrushes in different sizes
Primer
Topcoat
Wood stain
Varnish and waxes

I will talk more about paint and wood stain later in this chapter, and you can go to page 187 for more information on the different types and finishes of paint. When choosing paintbrushes, I try to avoid value packs as they tend not to be of great quality. I like to spend a little more on a good set of brushes and look after them. Taking the time to clean your brushes properly will make them last longer and give you a better paint job.

Power tools

Drill
Circular sander
Jigsaw
Mitre saw
Nail gun

You don't need to buy all of these power tools to begin with. Use what you have, or rent or borrow what you need, and build up your collection over time. Power tools do make the job easier, but if you're not confident at first, use a hand tool or ask for help. Make sure to read the user manual and safety guides before you begin, and start with small jobs.

Miscellaneous

Screwdriver set

Staple gun

Glue gun

Crafter's knives

Pliers

Screws and nails

Measuring tape and pencil

Hammer

Hand saw

Woodworking clamps

Remember to build your toolkit over time and invest in high-quality items as you need them. You will also need a small space to store your tools. You can use a toolbox, a storage box or some shelves in your shed or house. Mind your tools, and they will mind you!

Planning and Mood Boards

When I was an eager upcycling newbie, planning was a step I often skipped. I was so excited to get going that I didn't stop and think about how my new pieces would fit into the decor in my home. There are so many 'inspo' images and videos online that it's easy to become overwhelmed with ideas, and you might end up copying trends that don't stand the test of time.

I do love a unique and eclectic home stamped in personality, but mine was starting to look a bit mish-mashed! So now, before a paintbrush touches anything, I try to spend some time planning my colours and how I want a piece to look. I will share here some of my planning tips, which are also handy for general renovation projects.

How to find your style

I like to leave trends on the fashion runways! When it comes to your home, it should always shout 'you'. Our homes are our safe places, which we fill with treasure and trinkets we found along the way. If dark walls are trendy but you are a light and airy person, stick to lighter tones.

Inspiration is everywhere, from interior magazines to social media. I find the best inspiration when I am out and about. Coffee shops and hotels often have inspiring decor, and you can spend time there, figuring out how this particular style feels in real life.

On social media platforms, create boards to save any images that catch your eye. Don't overthink it or limit yourself to reality – have fun pulling down anything that you find attractive. Look through your chosen pictures for a common theme: Is there a distinctive colour palette? Or a pattern? Is it the styling I'm drawn to?

Create a mood board

When you have a rough idea of what you like, you can pull it together and create a mood board. If you're doing a larger project and decide to bring in an interior designer, this will be a really good starting point too.

You can create either a physical or a digital mood board. For a physical mood board, cut or print out images you like and place them together on a sheet of cardboard to create a collage. When you group these images together, you'll start to see your unique style.

You can create a digital mood board by using one of many free apps. A digital mood board is handy as you can have it on your phone and save images or items you see when out and about.

Identify the colours and patterns you are drawn to, as this will help you when picking paint shades for your upcycling projects. If you're drawn to a trendy or daring colour, consider painting just a small piece of furniture or bring it through with your accessories or soft furnishings.

Before taking the plunge and purchasing an item to upcycle, I ask myself these questions:

- Does the shape and size of this item fit in my home?
- Is it within my budget?
- Can I paint or change this piece to fit in with my style?
- What supplies will I need to achieve this look?

The goal of a mood board is to keep you on track when you are making decor decisions and hopefully help you to avoid making impulsive choices that could cost you more money down the line. It should be flexible and grow with you, just like your home.

Painting Furniture

I want you to get the most out of your lovely upcycled items, so let me share how I paint a piece of furniture. I always begin with good prep. Now, it's not as enjoyable as simply lashing on a few coats, but it means that your paint job will last longer and be less likely to chip.

Clean

Use a degreaser or warm, soapy water to clean your piece of furniture. You will be surprised how much dirt and oil comes off when rinsing. I like to use a sponge here, or a wire sponge if it's really heavy.

Sand

Using medium-grit sandpaper, I lightly sand the piece of furniture. You can sand by hand or with an electrical sander. Lightly sanding keys the surface and allows your primer and paint to get better adhesion. You don't have to sand the surface bare – just scratch the surface. Use a lint-free cloth to wipe away the dust before painting.

Prime

Choose a primer or undercoat. If a piece of furniture has never been painted or is bare wood, I recommend using a primer, which gives you a perfect base for your topcoat. Primers can also stop stains and oils from the wood from bleeding through to the surface. It's always good to use a shellac-based primer over dark wood and knotty pine.

If a piece of furniture has been painted previously, sand away any old, flaky paint and use an undercoat instead of a primer.

If you are painting a difficult surface such as tile or MDF, you can buy a specialist primer that will help paint to stick.

I use a small roller to apply one coat of primer. Generally, one is enough, but if you find you are getting stains bleeding through, then apply a second coat. Always check the back of the can for application guidelines.

Paint

Use a roller or brush to apply two coats of your chosen topcoat, whether it's a satin, matt or even an eggshell finish (see page 187 for more info). For most projects, two coats are plenty, but if the coverage looks

uneven or patchy, you can keep going. Always allow each coat of paint to dry before applying the next. Most topcoats are self-sealing and do not require varnish or wax. However, if using chalk paint – which on its own is hard to clean and could discolour – you will have to seal it with a clear varnish or clear wax.

Cure time

One of the most common reasons paint chips is because it hasn't had enough time to cure (become fully dry and durable). Although paint is touch-dry within a few hours, it needs a few days or even weeks to cure. Have you ever painted your nails and they smudge even though you thought they were dry? Well, it's the same for paint. Allow a week or so before using your piece of furniture, especially if it is a table or in a high-traffic area in your home.

Painting Flat-Pack Furniture

I see lots of flat-pack furniture down at the recycling centre. Often, these cheaper items are seen as disposable and end up in landfill once they're no longer needed. MDF and veneer finishes can be slightly harder to paint, but not impossible – I have lots of painted flat-pack items in my home, and their paint jobs have lasted very well.

I created this built-in effect storage wall with second-hand flat-pack pieces. Custom built-in furniture is popular at the moment, as it can give you lots of storage in a small space. I needed to store my ever-growing collection of craft supplies – I was getting tired of tripping over paint pots and sewing fabrics! – so this seemed like a budget-friendly and practical solution.

I already had a small storage unit in my office, and I got a free second-hand sideboard to use as the base. I decided to stack them to create the frame for my storage wall. When stacking or creating large walls like this, remember to anchor the furniture to the wall using brackets for safety. Ensure the wall you choose can bear the load of the furniture.

I used wood moulding from the hardware shop to add detail to the top, creating a custom built-in effect. To secure the moulding to the top, I used wood glue and my nail gun, and I then used decorators caulk to fill the joints and give it a seamless look.

Once I was happy with the base of my storage wall, it was time to prep the furniture pieces for paint. Here are my tips for getting the perfect paint finish on MDF and veneer finishes:

- Clean your furniture with a degreaser. Even if it looks and feels clean, there can be grease from fingerprints or unseen grime.
- Sand the surface. When painting MDF, which has such a smooth surface, this is an important step – you want to give the paint something to grip onto.
- Check for any damage and use a wood filler to patch up holes or chips.
- Choose a primer that has been designed for use on difficult surfaces such as MDF, UPVC and melamine.
- Once your primer is dry, apply two coats of your topcoat of choice. For my piece, I went for a satin finish as it's easy to clean. (See page 187 for other suggestions.)

If you're unsure about your choice of paint, test a small area first, making sure the primer has had twenty-four to forty-eight hours to dry beforehand.

The bottom sideboard I used had a previous paint job, so I needed to spend some time removing the old, flaky paint. Using an electric sander, I smoothed out old brush marks and got the surface as smooth as I could for painting. I also had to patch up old holes in the wood from the handles.

I used gold spray paint on all the handles to give them a uniform look. Some of the knobs are wooden and some metal, but you can't tell the difference, and it kept my budget down.

When you look at the 'before' image of the sideboard, I can see why many people would bring it to the recycle centre. However, I hope that the end result gives you the inspiration to rescue some flat-pack pieces and give them a new lease of life!

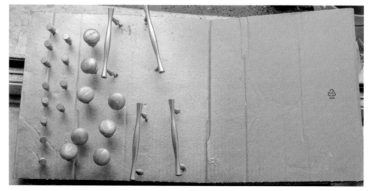

How to Strip Paint

There are many reasons why you may want to remove paint from a piece of furniture. Maybe you found a fab second-hand piece, but you don't like the paint job. Or maybe you made a mistake with your project, and you want to try again.

When I began upcycling, I put thick layers of white paint on everything. As I have gotten older and my style has evolved, I like the warmth and texture of wood. I also love playing with colour, and I have changed some of my white pieces to warm greens and pinks. By stripping pieces back and upcycling them many times, I have saved money and saved items from going to landfill.

I took some furniture upcycling classes as a beginner, and I noticed they gave us a lot of information about how to apply paint, but not so much about how to remove it. So I did a bit of research myself and learned how to strip back paint. It's not the sexiest of tasks, and a lot of elbow grease is required, but it's so rewarding to bring a piece back to life.

If you plan to repaint the piece of furniture, you can just follow the steps on page 118. Perform a good prep, remove any flaking paint and use an undercoat before applying your topcoat. However, if you want to bring a piece of furniture back to its bare wood, you can either use heat or chemical strippers.

Heat

- A heat gun looks like a hairdryer, but it's much more powerful. Heat guns work best on latex paint – I find they're not as good at removing chalk paint.

- Wearing protective gloves, start by applying heat in small areas. After a few seconds, you will notice the paint bubbling away from the surface. Using a scraper, gently lift off the old paint. Continue applying heat in small areas and scraping off until you get to the wood underneath.

- After you have removed the old paint, use a degreaser to give the piece a deep clean. Check the wood for any damage or areas that need repair. Use a sander or sanding block to smooth and even out the wood.

Chemical strippers

- In recent years, more environmentally friendly, water-based chemical strippers have come on the market. I find cheap chemical paint strippers hard to use, and they smell so strong that you need to use them in well-ventilated areas. Eco paint strippers take a little longer to work compared to the others, but they are easier to use. They're also very good with tricky chalk paint.

- Using a brush, apply a layer of paint stripper to the piece of furniture. Allow the stripper time to work

its magic, and you will start to notice the paint cracking and bubbling underneath.

- Use a scraper to remove the old paint. The stripper will leave a sticky residue, so I use a bucket of soapy water and a wire sponge to clean this off.

Tone and finish

- After stripping, if you like the wood underneath, you can apply an oil, wax or varnish to protect it. Another option is to use a wood stain to change the tone. With the rise in mid-century and boho decor, warm tones are popular these days, matched with texture and patterns.

When stripping furniture, always wear a mask and gloves to protect your skin and your lungs. With vintage furniture, there's a small chance the old paint could contain lead. Lead-based paint was banned from use in Ireland and the UK in 1992, but if you're unsure, buy a lead test kit and check it out first.

Fireplace Upcycle

In most living rooms, especially those in older homes, the fireplace is the main focal point. Fireplaces can be expensive to rip out and redo, but you can give them a facelift with some paint and patience.

When I moved into my house, there was a lot of orange-stained pine woodwork around the place. It's common in homes built in the late-1990s, but it made the rooms look smaller and darker. In my living room, there was a beautiful open fireplace. I loved the height of it and the size, just not the colour. The wood was of excellent quality, and it seemed a shame to waste it, so I decided to give it a makeover. Let me share how you can paint your wood fireplace surround too.

What you need

Degreaser or warm, soapy water
Sponges and rags
Medium-grit sandpaper
Paintbrush and roller set
Primer
Topcoat

- When picking paint for this project, it must be one that won't crack or peel from the heat of the fire. As you can see from the photos of my fireplace, the wood is a decent distance away from the open fire. I used a satin finish paint as well as a primer. I lit my open fire quite a bit this past winter and had no problems with heat damage, but if you're unsure, buy a small tester pot of paint and see how it wears after a few nights with the fire lighting. You can also reach out to paint brands directly to enquire if their paint is suitable.

- Let's start with prep. As mentioned in earlier projects, a bit of prep will give you a lasting finish and prevent chipping and peeling. Use a degreaser or warm, soapy water and a sponge to scrub the wood. Rinse off any excess residue.

- Using medium-grit sandpaper, lightly sand in the direction of the wood grain. Use a lint-free cloth to wipe away dust. You can tape off any edges and lay some drop cloths if you are a messy painter.

- Next, you want to prime. Primer gives your topcoat a great base to adhere to. It will also block stains from bleeding through, especially on pine surfaces. If your fireplace has knotty pine, I recommend using a shellac-based primer to stop the oils from the wood from bleeding.

- Use a roller to apply a thin coat of primer and a small paintbrush for hard-to-reach areas. Give the

primer time to dry before applying your topcoat.

- Apply two thin coats of your topcoat of choice, allowing the first to dry before applying the second. If using a satin, gloss or eggshell paint, these are self-sealing and do not require wax or varnish. If you have chosen a chalk paint, it will need a coat of wax or varnish to seal. I added a clay decorative moulding and painted it in the same shade.

- If you want to paint the inside of your firebox or stove, you will need a specialist paint that can withstand very high degrees of heat. This specialist paint mainly comes in black and is geared towards painting BBQs and stoves.

- Once you are happy with your paint job, give it a few days to cure. Your new fireplace will be wipeable and easy to clean. I painted mine over six years ago, and I only recently gave it a touch-up to change the colour. By following the steps here, you will have a long-lasting paint job that you can admire as you warm your feet on chilly winter nights.

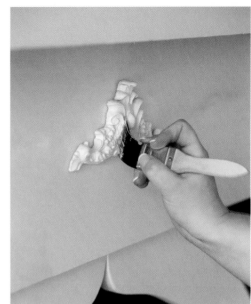

Kitchen Cabinets Makeover

For me, the kitchen is the heart of a home – it's the first place everyone gathers in my house. The kettle works overtime and the tea is always flowing in an Irish kitchen.

Before I bought my home, I dreamed of having a cottage kitchen, one that was light and airy and full of charm and character. In reality, when I started looking at houses, I realised that my budget would only stretch to brown MDF cabinets and 'previously lived-in' charm! But there's always a way to make it your own, so I decided to paint the cabinets. I have painted them again since, and they are currently a lovely warm shade of pink.

Painting your cabinets is a budget-friendly way to transform your kitchen, and it let me have the feel a cottage kitchen without spending a huge amount.

What you need

Degreaser or warm, soapy water
Sponges and rags
Medium-grit sandpaper
Drop cloths
Paintbrush and roller set
Primer
Topcoat

- When choosing a paint finish (see page 187) for kitchen cabinets, I recommend satin or eggshell. These are durable in high-traffic areas, and you can easily clean them with warm, soapy water. Chalk and matt paint are not as durable, and the finishing waxes can look dirty over time.

- As mentioned in previous projects, it's worth taking the time to prep a good base for your topcoat. Kitchen cabinets can have a lot of unseen grime. Use a tough degreaser to remove built-up oil.

- You can unscrew the cabinet doors and paint them on a flat surface if you find that easier – it will also give you a tidy, professional finish. I removed my doors and cleaned them in the bath.

- Use medium-grit sandpaper to lightly sand the wood on each cabinet door. Use a lint-free cloth to wipe away dust.

- Tape the edges for a tidy paint job and lay drop cloths to protect your countertops and kitchen floor.

- Use a roller set to apply a thin coat of primer. Applying thin coats will prevent drips and give you a more even finish. Use a paintbrush for hard-to-reach areas. A little tip: I used an old makeup brush on my kitchen cabinets as it gave a smoother finish than a normal paintbrush.

- If you are painting over previously painted kitchen cabinets, you can prepare the surface as mentioned above and use an undercoat instead of a primer. If your cabinets have a shiny veneer finish, use a specialist primer.

- Allow the primer time to dry before applying your topcoat.

- Apply two thin coats of your chosen topcoat, allowing the first to dry before applying the second. Don't worry if the first coat is patchy and uneven – the magic happens when you paint that second coat.

- Once your paint is dry, allow it a few days to cure. The paint will harden, making it durable and easy to clean.

- Another lovely way to upcycle and put your own stamp on your kitchen cabinets is by changing the hardware. You can find loads of funky hardware online that won't break the bank. Search on second-hand sites for handles or knobs, as many people sell these on.

- Now that you've created fresh new kitchen cabinets without spending a heap of money, maybe it's time to change your tiles or get a new worktop. Have fun making your dream kitchen a reality!

When cleaning painted cabinets, use warm, soapy water rather than harsh cleaning products that may weaken the paint. Once when I was cleaning my oven, some of the foam dropped onto my cabinet and lifted off the paint. Luckily I had some paint in the shed for a touch-up!

Skirting and Architraves

Painting your skirting boards or architraves (that is, the moulded frames around doors or windows) can make a massive difference to a room, making it feel bigger, brighter and more spacious. Coloured trim is popular these days, with many people painting their wood trim the same shade as their walls. Whether you are fond of white skirting or you love a pop of colour, let me share some tips for painting your internal woodwork. I suggest doing this project by degrees, room by room, as it can be a bit of a back-breaking job.

When choosing a topcoat, I recommend any satin, eggshell or gloss finish paint. I know gloss white skirting boards are a bit dated, but they're very durable. Have a flick over to page 187 for help deciding on a topcoat.

Painting over paint

If you live in an older home, it is always a good idea to test for lead in the old paint. It is also likely that the old layer of paint may be oil-based; for the new layer, I'm going to recommend water-based paint. Oil-based paints are less kind to the environment, smell strong and are higher in Volatile Organic Compounds (VOCs) than water-based paints. They also tend to discolour and go yellow over time, as the oils bleed within the paint. Oil-based paints are known for being durable and long-lasting; however, as long as you do some prep, your new water-based paint should be just as good. Water- and oil-based paints don't bond well together, but again, with the correct prep, you shouldn't have a problem painting over the old layer.

What you need

Degreaser
Cloths
Fine-grit sandpaper
Tack cloths
Drop cloths
Tape
Paintbrushes
Primer
Topcoat

- First, you need to deep-clean the surface to remove grime and dirt.
- Use fine-grit sandpaper to sand the old paint. You are not trying to remove it, just to sand the surface until it's no longer glossy.
- Wipe away any dust from sanding with a tack cloth.
- Lay drop cloth to protect your floor and use painter's tape on edges for a tidy finish.
- Apply one coat of primer. When painting over oil-based paint, choose a primer for difficult surfaces.
- Apply two coats of your chosen topcoat.
- If you are painting over new wood, follow the same steps as above. Use a primer to stop oils and sap from the wood from bleeding, as this will prevent your paint job from discolouring over time.
- Whilst it might seem like a lot of work, taking time to properly prep will give you a long-lasting and durable finish. It'll be worth it!

Dreamy Dollhouse

When I was little, I dreamed of owning a fancy dollhouse. However, I was a child in the 1990s in Ireland, so I had to settle for a plastic Wendy house and some DIY dollhouses from cereal boxes. Maybe having to use my imagination at a young age planted the seeds for my creative upcycles in adulthood!

My love of dollhouses stayed with me, and a few years ago I decided to look for a second-hand one to make over for my niece. I set search alerts on buy-and-sell websites, and eventually the perfect one popped up. It was from a local seller – the family was doing a toy clear-out before Christmas. So, one man's junk became another lady's treasure!

What you need

Dollhouse
Degreaser
Cloths
Cotton swabs
Primer
Topcoat
Toy furniture
Dollhouse flooring
Lollipop sticks
Glue

- I began by thoroughly cleaning the dollhouse, inside and out, with a degreaser. It had many hard-to-reach areas, so I removed the front panels for easier access. Cotton swabs also came in handy.

- My dollhouse was made of wood, so I applied one coat of primer inside and out. I allowed that to fully dry before applying the topcoat.

- I consulted with my niece on the topcoat colour, and we agreed on pink! I applied two coats of light-pink paint in a satin finish to the outside of the dollhouse. When painting toys or kids' furniture, choose a paint that's low in VOCs and marked as suitable for children's items.

- For the inside of the dollhouse, I went for lighter shades of paint. Tester pots are handy for smaller projects, and you will save on paint costs. Painting the inside of the dollhouse was tricky – I used old makeup brushes with small bristles to make the job easier.

- Styling the house was the fun part! I wanted to create a pretty interior, and since it was for my niece, I bought lots of toy furniture – rather than collectors' dollhouse furniture – to bring her joy and endless playtime.

- I chose a herringbone floor for the inside. The flooring was a thick sheet of paper, which I cut to size for each room and glued down with wood glue. I bought it online – there are so many niche sites that cater to dollhouses.

- To create the faux panelling in the living room, I used lollipop sticks. I carefully measured the room before cutting the lollipop sticks to size. I applied glue to the wood sticks and stuck them to the walls before painting them.

- Using toy furniture, I dressed out each room. My inner child was so happy! The toy furniture was age-appropriate for my niece, and I was able to get some of it second-hand.

- This project was a labour of love, and it took me some time to complete it. Not every upcycle you do will be a weekend job – some need more time. So, enjoy the process and fall in love with the journey!

Chapter Five

Let Yourself Bloom

There is magic in gardening. Not only is it relaxing, but it is another way to express your creativity. Gardening makes me feel grounded, still and calm. There is something about touching soil, having muck under my fingernails, that gives me joy. It also teaches me to be patient: just plant the seed, give it the correct soil and the right conditions, and wait. Sometimes it's easy to forget that we need to do this in our own lives too.

Another lesson the garden has taught me is that, like a flower, we all have our seasons. We live in a 24/7 world, where we feel the need to be 'on' all the time. But by nature, there are times when we are in bloom and times when we need to retreat, rest and let our leaves fall away. Ask yourself, what are my seasons? Have I been trying to be 'on' all the time? Are there ways I can let go?

In this section, I will share some of my favourite projects to help you get inspired to head into your garden, whether it's a tiny terrace or a plentiful patch.

Gardening Essentials

Many people would love to get gardening but don't know where to start. I remember how confusing it all was in the beginning. I didn't understand the difference between an annual or a perennial – I would be disheartened when a flower died and surprised to see it come back to life the following season!

One lovely thing about gardening is that you don't need a lot of space; you can create a beautiful container garden in a small pocket of your home with just a pot, some soil, water and seeds.

Here are some gardening terms that will help you choose the right flowers and plants for your gardening projects.

Perennial vs Annual

An annual plant will last for one growing season. You can plant annuals from seeds in spring and once the risk of frost has passed, you can replant outside. An annual will bloom and produce seeds before completing its life cycle – so basically, these guys die off at the end of the season.

A perennial plant will come back again each year. They start to grow in spring or summer. They bloom when they are supposed to, and then they die back – usually with the first frost of autumn – to return the following year.

Just to confuse you, some plants are biennials. A biennial is a flowering plant that has a two-year biological cycle. In the first year, it will produce roots, stems and some foliage. In the second year, it will grow flowers, fruit and seeds, depending on the plant. Most biennials will reseed, and then the parent plant usually dies. Some common garden biennials are foxgloves and dianthus.

I like to use annuals in pots and containers to add colour to my garden during the spring and summer. I plant perennials in my flowerbeds and propagate (that is, breed) them every few seasons to get more plants.

When to plant

Be patient and think ahead. If you want spring flowers, plant them around October time. For summer/autumn flowers from bulbs or seed, plant them around May. Planting timelines will be different for every growing zone, and these are just rough timelines: always check the back of your seed or bulb packet for information on when to plant. Try not to plant seeds or young plants outside until late May, when the risk of frost has passed. You can keep the seedlings in the kitchen or greenhouse at first and then transplant them into larger containers or flower beds a few months later.

Cutting

It is common to hear people talking about taking or sharing 'cuttings'. A cutting is a section of your plant that is capable of developing into a new plant. It's a great and inexpensive way to get more plants for your garden. The most popular cuttings are from stem and root.

Stem cuttings are when you snip a piece of stem from the mother plant and place it part-buried in soil, leaving at least one leaf node. Over time, the cutting can produce new roots, usually at the node.

Root cuttings are when a section of the cutting root is buried just below the soil surface, and the cutting produces new shoots.

Deadheading

Deadheading means removing dead flower heads from your plants. For example, when my daffodils finish flowering, I remove the dead flowering heads and let the stems go yellow – this allows all the energy and goodness to go back into the bulb for next year – and then cut away the old foliage. Dead-heading annuals controls the spread of seeds and encourages the plant to create more flowers.

Drainage

I have fallen victim to soggy pots and buckets and learnt the hard way about the importance of proper drainage! If your soil is too wet and starts to flood, your plant can suffer from mould or die off, and the root can rot if it sits in a pool of water. Make sure there are some holes at the bottom of your pot to allow excess water to escape.

You can also add perlite or sharp sand to your soil for extra drainage. Some plants require more drainage than others; whenever I buy a new plant or seed, I try to read up on the kind of soil that species would prefer.

Propagating

A great way to save money in the garden is to propagate existing plants – essentially, grow new plants for free. To propagate a plant, you can collect seed, take cuttings (see page 142) or divide rootballs. Some plants are more difficult to propagate than others, but it is always worth trying.

Transplanting

Transplanting is when you move a fully grown seedling or mature plant to a new location. If you had seedlings in the kitchen during the colder months, you can then transplant them to larger pots or flower beds. If a plant is not performing well in one area of your garden, you can transplant it to somewhere more suitable.

When transplanting seedlings, be very gentle with the stems. Lift your seedlings by their leaves and carefully place them in their new location, making sure to not firm the roots down too much as you don't want to damage them.

How to plant

Planting sounds easy, but it can be tricky. When I started gardening, I would often dig a hole that was too shallow, resulting in an unhappy (or dead) plant. Make sure to dig a hole that is both wide and deep enough for the plant roots. The same rule applies to pots – choose ones that will give your plant some room to grow.

If moving a plant from a pot, gently tease out the tips of the roots using your fingers before placing it in the hole or new pot.

After placing your plant or bulb in the soil, carefully fill in loose dirt around the roots until the hole is full. Pat the soil down to eliminate any gaps or trapped air. Don't pack the soil too much, but it does need to be solid enough to support the plant and hold the roots in place.

When to water

Some plants require more water than others, and rainwater is always best. If you have space for a water butt in your garden, you can collect rainwater for your indoor and outdoor plants.

I try to keep the soil moist in pots and containers, as these dry out the quickest. For garden borders, I water when the weather is dry and hot – how often depends on the climate where you live. My best tip for watering is: Don't assume that your plant is getting enough water just because it has rained. Some plants, especially those in pots, can grow in a way that stops the rain from touching the soil. Always make sure to water the soil and not the leaves.

No-Dig Raised Bed

When it comes to gardening, I am still quite an amateur. I have grown wonky carrots in pots and used many random containers in my growing experiments! But as my thumb got greener, I realised I could do with more growing space in my garden. A raised bed – which is essentially a box made of wood, filled with enough soil to support plants without touching the soil underneath – gives you extra space and is easy to customise to your needs and to the size of your garden.

Research suggests that growing in raised beds is better for the environment than digging up the ground: under our feet in the soil, there are already billions of fungal threads, nematodes and earthworms working away, and by not digging the earth, we can leave them undisturbed and help them continue their work. Also, if your soil is not great, creating raised beds means you can get the soil right and have a better chance at a successful crop.

What you need

Long strips of wood treated for outdoor use
Measuring tape, pencil and ruler
Hand saw or circular saw
Protective gloves
Protective eyewear
Power drill
Screws for outdoor use
Cardboard
Shovel
Wheelbarrow
Topsoil
Peat-free compost
Vermiculite or sharp sand
Sieve

Choose the right spot

Pick an area in your garden that gets a balance of sun and shade. Take some time to research the plants you would like to grow and how much sun they need, and this will give you an idea of the best spot to place them. When positioning your raised beds, leave enough of a gap between them for walking and mowing the grass.

Create the frame

- My raised beds are 6 x 3 ft (180 x 90 cm) and 14 in (36 cm) deep – you can customise these measurements to fit your own garden space. Having a nice depth gives you more options for growing, as rooted plants like carrots need that extra space. If you are not confident cutting wood or choosing the correct timber, you can purchase DIY kits online.

- Carefully measure and mark where you want to cut your wood using a hand saw or a circular saw. Use protective gloves and eyewear for this part.

    Cut four pieces of wood 6 ft x 7 in (180 x 18 cm)

    Cut four pieces of wood 3 ft x 7 in (90 x 18 cm)

    Cut four 14 in (36 cm) long posts of wood for the corners

- Assemble your frame by screwing the 3 ft pieces of wood to the corner posts first. Once you have the two smaller sides screwed into the post, screw the longer pieces of wood to the corner posts.

Position and fill your bed

- Bring your raised bed frame to your preferred spot in the garden.

- You want to line the bottom of the raised bed with a barrier to prevent the grass or weeds from growing up. I laid layers of cardboard; you can also use straw, bark or landscape fabric.

- You can now fill the beds with soil. I used a shovel and wheelbarrow to fill my two beds with 1 tonne of soil. Topsoil is great, and you can often get it for free if you search online, but it may lack nutrients so it's important to add peat-free compost to the mix. Make sure to sieve the topsoil to remove stones.

- Now for the fun part! Planting. Whether you grow cut flowers or vegetables, feel proud knowing that you are making a positive impact on your environment. The pollinators will be very grateful for all these new plants!

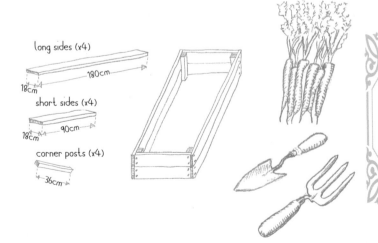

long sides (x4)

180cm

18cm

short sides (x4)

90cm

18cm

corner posts (x4)

36cm

If you are a newbie like me, you can order pre-mixed soil from larger garden supply shops. It contains screened topsoil, peat-free compost, and horticultural sand and grit for drainage.

Raised Bed with Legs

If you're short on space in your garden or struggle to work at a low height, why not try making a raised garden bed? A raised bed is particularly good for growing vegetables, herbs and flowers. I had resisted growing vegetables for many years as I thought I needed a big patch, but as it turns out, lots of varieties grow happily in small containers.

I created this raised garden bed for growing carrots. When I first sowed carrots, I learned that the seedlings needed to be thinned out and transplanted into more generous garden beds or containers. I also learned that carrots don't like to be disturbed. I had a very wonky carrot harvest that first year! Nowadays, I wait until the ground is warm and sow them directly into the raised bed or a container. That is the magic of gardening – you are always learning, and there is no such thing as perfection!

What you need

Long strips of wood treated for outdoor use
Narrow pieces of wood for the legs
Measuring tape, pencil and ruler
A saw or power saw
A drill
Screws for outdoor use
Wood glue (optional)
Wire mesh
Weed prevention fabric

Create the frame

- I purchased long strips of wood from my local building providers, which I then cut to size. My raised bed is 31.5 in (80 cm) long, 22 in (56 cm) wide, and the legs are 31.5 inches (80 cm) tall. The planks of wood I bought were 6 in (15 cm) deep, so I stacked them two on top of each other, giving my raised bed an overall depth of 12 in (30 cm). I have three legs on either side. Feel free to customise and adjust the measurements to suit your needs.

- Using your measuring tape and a ruler, measure your wood pieces and mark with a pencil where you need to cut. Carefully use your saw to cut the wood. You may find it easier to use a power tool here, and if you're nervous you should ask someone to cut the wood pieces for you.

- Attach the legs to the side panels. Use your drill to make a pilot hole before screwing the screw into

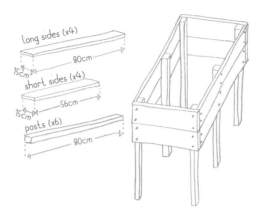

long sides (x4)
80cm
15cm
short sides (x4)
56cm
15cm
posts (x6)
80cm

the wood. For extra security, I like to apply a bead of glue to the wood before screwing it. Don't worry if glue bleeds out over the sides – you can wipe this away. I attached a third leg to the middle of the side to support the weight of the garden bed.

• Once you have the side pieces assembled, attach the two shorter sides. You may need someone to hold the pieces for you as you drill them together.

Lining and filling your bed

• Once you have created the frame, attach the wire mesh to the base. I fixed mine in place with lots of screws, as the bed can get heavy with the weight from the soil.

• Line the bed with some garden fabric. I used a leftover weed membrane. This will stop the soil from falling out and help with drainage.

• Position your new garden bed in the spot you would like to keep it before adding your soil. Use a mix of peat-free compost, organic matter and vermiculite to create the perfect soil to grow your vegetables in.

• Have fun sowing your veg! My raised bed has evolved over time and is now a home for herbs. Do some experimenting to see what grows best in your space.

Painting Outdoors

Nothing makes me smile more than a pop of colour in the garden. In winter, when all the plants are sleeping, I love to look out my kitchen window and see some brightness.

A great way to add some colour is by painting a fence, a shed or a wall. If you already have plenty of colour in your plants and shrubs, you may only need one colourful feature to complement the landscape instead of taking away from it. I'll also show you how to paint a piece of wooden garden furniture, which could be a chair, a table or a bench; in a family garden, you could brighten up a sandbox, a swing or a mud kitchen.

Painting garden furniture

- Before painting, deep-clean your wooden furniture with a degreaser. I like to power-wash my pieces, but a bucket of warm, soapy water and a wire sponge will do the trick. Use the wire sponge to scrub away mould, moss and algae before rinsing off all residue.

- Allow your garden furniture to dry fully; painting over damp wood can cause mould. While it is tempting to get out and paint on the first sunny day of the year, check the weather – you want to be sure of a few warm days in a row, as some paint takes longer to dry and cure in low temperatures.

- Assess for damage. If the item is rotting in places, see if it is worth the cost of repair versus buying a new one. If the wood is crumbling or weakened or shows signs of woodworm, this may be a safety hazard.

- If your furniture has been previously painted, use a scraper to remove flakes. Take the time to remove as much of the old paint as you can.

- Lightly sand with a medium-grit sanding block to smooth the wood and prepare for adhesion. This is especially important for previously painted surfaces. Some outdoor paints contain oils, so if you paint over the wood without preparing it, the paint may not adhere well.

- I recommend buying specialist outdoor paint, which you'll find in the outdoor aisle of most hardware shops, as it has built-in UV filters and other components to make it weather-hardy.

- Apply your outdoor paint, allowing plenty of time to dry between coats.

- While it can be tempting to use your freshly painted piece straight away, allow it time to cure, especially if it is a chair or a table.

- If you're painting a large surface like a fence or a shed, I recommend investing in an electric paint sprayer. I bought mine online for less than €50 when repainting my shed – it was much quicker and saved my aching hands. For smaller, hard-to-reach areas, use good-quality paintbrushes and rollers. Special fence brushes are great for painting large panels, as you can work the paint into the wood grain, and you have more control.

- Whether you choose a sprayer or a brush, lay some drop cloth and tape any edges before painting, as this will give you a tidy, professional finish.

Painting exterior walls

- When I first moved into my home, I had a pebble-dashed wall that had turned grey, and no amount of power-washing could save it! I decided to paint it white, and it gave my garden the lovely, cottage feel I was looking for.

- To prepare a wall for painting, use a wire brush and a scraper to remove old, flaking paint. If there is fungus or algae present, you may need to power-wash or treat your walls.

- Lay a drop cloth to protect your path from paint drips and tape up any areas for a tidy paint finish.

- Use an outdoor masonry brush to apply two coats of masonry paint. While it can be tempting to purchase cheaper paint, it won't last as long and may cost you more in the long run. A good masonry paint will last for up to five years or more before needing a recoat. Allow your paint to dry fully between coats.

Tyre Planter

Millions of car tyres become unusable each year – they're difficult to recycle as they contain metals and chemicals that are harmful to the environment when burnt. You can pick them up for a few euro (or free) on second-hand websites. Some gardeners use tyres to make raised beds in their borders, which is a great idea. Another lovely way to repurpose one is to create a planter for your garden.

It is believed the chemicals from tyres only release when they are burnt or slowly over time; still, I prefer to use my tyre for annuals and perennials rather than edible plants like herbs and vegetables. For the past few years, I have a wildflower mix thriving in my tyre planter. It makes a pretty floral display and provides food for the bees and other insects.

What you need

Two tyres
Power washer (optional)
Wire brush and soapy water
Piece of wood
Jigsaw or hand saw
Drill
Screws suitable for outdoor use
Legs or castors (optional)
Recycled plastic

- Choose two tyres of the same size. Before turning them into planters, give the tyres a deep clean. A blast of a power washer is ideal, but you can also use a wire brush and warm, soapy water to remove any built-up grime and grease.
- To create a base, trace the round shape of the tyre onto a piece of wood. Carefully cut the wood using a jigsaw or hand saw.
- Drill the wooden base into the rubber tyre using a drill and screws. Drill a hole in the base to create drainage in your planter.
- You can add legs or castor wheels to your planter to raise it off the ground. You can stack two tyres, as I did, or you can use only one. If stacking the tyres, secure them to each other by screwing the inner walls of each tyre together.
- Use recycled plastic to line the planter and protect the wood from rotting. I used old plastic bags – just

make sure to check them for holes beforehand.

• Fill with a mix of peat-free compost, organic matter and add some vermiculite or grit for drainage. Have fun with your floral display. Why not plant some tulips and daffodils for spring colour, or some dahlias for a late summer or early autumn bloom?

Teacup Bird Feeders

If you have spare bits of mismatched china, why not use them to serve some seeds to the birds in your garden? I love to leave food out for my local birdies and watch them play from my kitchen window. It helps to sustain the wild birds through the winter months, and in return, they'll you help out. I've noticed the smaller birds eating insects and aphids off my roses and plants – since they keep the bugs under control, I don't have to use any pesticides.

When you start feeding birds in your garden, you will notice the many species that live amongst us. I have a robin who visits, and he prefers to eat the seed that falls on the ground. Other smaller birds like the blue tit and chaffinch happily swing and eat from bird feeders. Having a mix of tables and feeders will cater to most birds native to your area.

What you need

A china cup and a plate
Strong glue adhesive
Tape
Strong twine or chain
Metal hooks

- When choosing china, the lighter the better. Check for cracks or chips, as these could injure a bird's leg or claw. Wash your teacups well to remove grime.
- The glue is the essential part of this project. Choose adhesive that requires time to set. You want it to be strong enough to hold the weight of the plate, seed and bird. I like to use E6000 or Gorilla Glue.

- Position the cup in the centre of the saucer, on its side. Apply a bead of glue to the saucer and firmly place the cup on top. Use some tape to hold the cup and saucer together while the glue cures.

- You can sit the teacup feeder on a shelf, or you can hang it. To hang, add either a sturdy piece of twine or a thin metal chain to the handle of your cup. The string shouldn't be too long – around five or six inches, depending on what you're hanging it from – as we don't want the teacup to over-swing or blow around too much in the wind. Add a hook to a wall or a wooden palette like mine and hang your bird feeder from it. You can also hang it from the branch of a tree.

- It is best to keep your teacup feeders in a sheltered area, away from harsh winds and weather. Check your feeders regularly for any sign of deterioration and clean them with warm water to help stop the spread of disease and bacteria.

- It may take a week or more for the birds to discover your new feeders, but when they do, I promise that you will have some regular visitors to your garden.

To make a sturdier teacup feeder, instead of using glue, you can drill a hole of the same size in both the cup and plate, then use a screw and nut to secure the cup to the plate. Head to page 99 and follow the steps for drilling through china.

Garden Chair Shelf

Along with being unable to resist teacups, I have a thing for chairs too! Chairs are great for upcycling, as you can paint them, reupholster them, turn them into shelves or recycle the wood. And you can always find a lonely chair in a second-hand shop or online.

If you come across a broken chair, remember that it's often good for more than just firewood. I had a chair with a broken leg, and I decided to turn it into a shelf for my garden. For this project, you will need to do some cutting, but it is a relatively simple DIY, and it will add interest and fun to your outdoor space.

What you need

A wooden chair
A hand saw or electric saw
Protective eyewear and gloves
A scrap piece of wood
A drill
Screws
L-shaped brackets
Degreaser
Sandpaper
Outdoor paint and varnish
Brackets
Wall plug

- Begin by cutting the top of the chair from the bottom seat. I cut right at the base where the spindles were. Carefully cut the wood with a hand saw, wearing gloves and protective eyewear. You can also use electric power tools for a quicker job, and a jigsaw would do the trick. Secure the chair before cutting to get a safe, straight cut.

- You will use just the top of the chair for this DIY, so put aside the base for now. I will share further down how I used it to create a planter.

- To create a shelf, cut a scrap piece of wood slightly wider than the chair frame. Secure it to the top of the chair by using an L-shaped bracket. Use your drill to drill a pilot hole, then screw in screws to secure the bracket to the wood.

- Once you are happy with your shelf, it is time to paint.

- Use a degreaser to clean the wood and remove grime and dirt. Lightly sand the wood to key the piece before painting and wipe away any dust from sanding.

- Use outdoor paint here, as this will protect your shelf and prevent the wood from deteriorating. Depending on the brand you choose, you may need to prime. For extra protection, you can apply a layer of clear varnish, like a yacht varnish. Always check the instructions on the back of the tin, and check out page 153 for more info on painting outdoor furniture.
- Attach your shelf to a wall by using brackets. If it's a concrete wall, you'll need to use a drill with a hammer function and a masonry drill bit. Insert a wall plug into the holes and screw in your brackets. Use brackets big enough to take the weight of the shelf and any pots you may place on it.
- I like to display small pots on my shelves, and I secure them with a tiny bit of velcro so they won't blow over. It's best to position your new shelf in a sheltered spot, to protect it from the wind.

Planter

- To transform the base of the chair into a planter, you will need a staple gun and some hessian or weed liner.
- Remove the seat pad from the base of the chair. On my chair, there was a frame that held the legs which had a gap in the middle. I created a 'pot' out of weed liner and used my staple gun to staple it around the base. To make it deep, I pushed the material down.
- Once all was secure, I added some compost. As it's quite shallow, it's perfect for annual plants like violas or pansies. Keep them well fed and watered, and they will bloom until the first frost.

Gorgeous Garden Pillows

On a trip to Morocco, I noticed how well they used rugs, cushions and pillows in their homes. If you are short on space in your garden, you can use soft furnishings to create a place to hang out on the rare days when we have some sunshine! I love to throw a rug onto the grass and plop some pillows out to create a space to relax with friends. This set-up is also perfect for an at-home outdoor cinema experience. Large garden pillows can be expensive, so let me show you how to make your own using lightweight rugs. If you don't have a sewing machine, these can be sewn by hand with a large needle and thick thread.

What you need

Lightweight woven rugs
Cotton or poly-cotton fabric
Sewing pins
Pillows for the filler
Sewing machine and thread

- I got my rugs new for a few euro each, but you can also check second-hand shops and sites. For the fabric on the back, you can recycle an old pillowcase or use any spare cotton or poly-cotton.
- Gather your materials and iron your backing fabric so it is smooth and crease-free.
- Cut the backing fabric to the same width and length as the rug. Place the materials together, with the right sides facing each other. You can add pins to keep the fabric in place when you are sewing.
- Straight stitch down the two sides of your material. Make sure to do a backstitch at the start and end

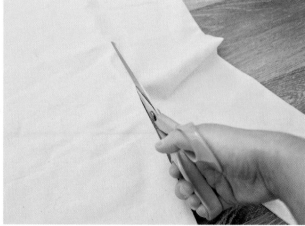

of your stitching, to make it secure and stop it from unravelling. As the fabric is heavier, you may need to use a thicker thread to avoid snapping. You can also adjust the length of your stitch to make it easier. Always use a sharp needle on your machine when sewing, as a blunt needle may snap or snag the fabric.

- Reverse your cushion inside out. The right side of the fabric will now face you. You can iron your seams flat too. Stitch one of the openings closed by folding the cotton backing fabric over to create a seam, and straight stitch it down to close the bottom of the pillow.

- Now you can insert your pillows as filler. I inserted two as one wasn't making it as full as I wanted it to be.

- Close the opening by folding over the backing fabric, like the other seam, and straight-stitch down the fabric. Another option would be to stitch velcro to the opening – that would mean you could remove the inserts and pop the cover into the washing machine.

- Throw some rugs onto the grass, layer your newly made pillows and get cosy. I love to pop a tray in the middle of the rug for snacks and share the garden experience with my friends (or the cats!).

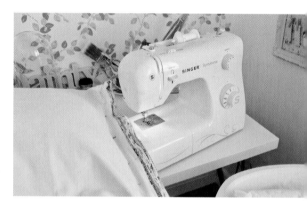

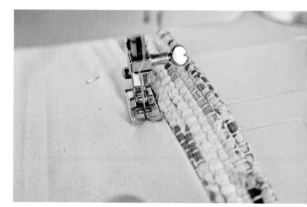

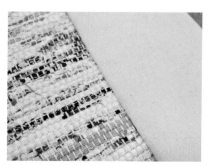

DIY Garden Apron

When pottering in the garden and doing my jobs, I never seemed to have anywhere to hold my stuff. I love listening to podcasts or music and switching off from the real world, but my phone was forever falling out of my pocket and taking my earphones with it! So I decided to make myself a handy half apron just for gardening.

Here's how I made mine, and you can adjust and customise it: add extra pockets, make the pockets deeper or longer, and tweak them to suit you and whatever you need while outdoors.

What you need

Cotton or poly-cotton fabric
Iron
Measuring tape and ruler
Fabric marker or tailor's chalk
Fabric scissors
Sewing machine
Thread

- For the apron, there are three parts: the body, the pockets and the straps. Here are the dimensions I used for mine, but use your measuring tape to gauge how wide and long you would like it:

  Body: 20 in (50 cm) wide x 15 in (38 cm) long. Cut 1 piece

  Pocket: 16 in (40 cm) wide x 9 in (23 cm) long. Cut 1 piece

  Straps: 4 in (10 cm) wide x 30 in (76 cm) long. Cut 2 pieces

- Iron your material before cutting. Using your fabric marker and ruler, draw your measurements for the three pieces onto the fabric, then use your fabric scissors to cut the pieces out.

- Begin by making the straps. Fold the right sides (patterned sides) of your strap in half and iron. Straight stitch the side of the strap but leave one of the openings open.

- Pull the fabric right side out – a safety pin might help with this part – and iron. Topstitch down both sides of the straps to get a tidy finish.

- Now on to the body. Use your iron to fold the raw edge of the fabric back ½ an inch, then fold again to create a hem. Use lots of pins to secure in place if you are a sewing newbie.

- Before sewing the hem, tuck your apron straps into the body. Measure how far up you would like your apron strings to be and pin them in place. Double-check that they are equal on both sides.

- Tuck the straps into the hem, and then fold it back on itself and secure it with a pin.
- Take the body to the machine and topstitch all the way around. When sewing over the straps, you can do a backstitch to give them extra reinforcement.
- For the pocket, begin by hemming the top of the material. Use your iron to fold the raw edge over, then over again and topstitch on your machine.
- Use your iron to fold over the raw edge on the remaining three sides of the pocket. Find the middle of your body and pin the pocket into place. Before stitching around the three sides, check that the pocket is even and in the best position for you.
- Topstitch the three sides of the pocket onto the body. To divide up your larger pocket into smaller ones and add sections, do a line of stitching. Measure across and decide how wide you would like the pocket, then do a line of topstitching from the bottom to the top of the pocket. May your seed packets never fly away and your bits and bobs remain in order with your lovely new apron!

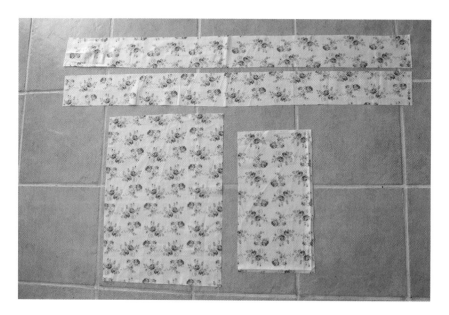

Herbal Tea Garden

My philosophy is: grow the plants you will use the most in your garden. If you're not bothered with vegetables, why not try planting herbs that you can use for cooking and making teas and oils? Some herbs grow effortlessly in pots and containers, so there's no need to dig raised beds. However, you can grow larger plants in borders or beds that also give beautiful flowers. I love the echinacea in my garden – you can dry it for tea but also enjoy the pretty plant when it blooms within the border.

What to grow

You'd be surprised how many herbs and plants you can use for making tea and essential oils. In my garden, I grow lemon balm, sage, mint, calamintha, chamomile, verbena, fennel, echinacea, heuchera and lavender.

Lavender, echinacea, verbena and fennel can grow quite large. When this happens, you can transplant them into larger pots or create a flower bed. They are perennial, so they come back each year.

Lemon balm, sage and mint can be grown in medium-sized terracotta pots. Just remember that clay pots dry out quicker, so make sure to keep the soil moist. I tried growing mint in my raised flower bed and found that it can be a bit invasive, so I suggest keeping it in a pot instead, so it doesn't take over the border.

Chamomile has a beautiful flower which can be used in arrangements, and it will grow well with mint and basil in a herb garden.

How to dry flowers and herbs for tea

There are many ways to dry herbs and flowers. I will share tips for air drying, which is free and easy, but other methods include using a dehydrator, a microwave and an oven. The best time to pick flowers and herbs from your garden is around mid-morning, when the dew has dried but before the sun dries the oils within your plant. It is better to use flowers from your garden rather than shop-bought flowers, as these may have pesticides and chemicals on them to prolong their life.

Gather your herbs or flowers and wash them thoroughly. Remove any foliage from the stems. Take a small piece of string and tie the stems together tightly. Hang the bunch upside down for drying. Place it in a greenhouse or in direct sunlight – above a window in your home is perfect. Rotate the bunch every so often. Alternatively, you can remove the flower heads you want to air-dry from the stems and place them on a tray to dry, again in a sunny spot.

How long the herbs and flowers take to dry out depends on both temperature and humidity; the lower

the humidity in the air, the quicker they will dry. Warm and dry is best. Most herbs will dry out in about ten days to two weeks.

Check your flowers and herbs often. They should crumble and break easily in your hands when dry. When they are completely dried out, you can store them in an airtight container. Check the container for condensation, which can lead to mould – if you notice any condensation, remove the flowers and allow them to dry some more.

Herbal teas contain vitamins and antioxidants that are great for your health, but keep in mind that they should be consumed in reasonable amounts. Like all things in life, balance!

Creating your brew

You can use fresh or dried herbs and flowers for your tea, whatever you prefer. Add one or two teaspoons to your cup, in a tea infuser, fill with boiling water and wait for a while until the flavour sinks in. (A tea infuser will help you get the perfect brew.) You can add some lemon to enhance the flavour, or some honey if you like a sweeter taste. Some mornings, I pull fresh mint from the garden and pop it into a teapot so I can start the day with a fresh mint tea. It's also delicious in mojitos after the sun goes down!

Buzzin' Bee Hotel

Did you know that some shop-bought bee hotels can do more harm than good? If they're not properly maintained and checked for mites, mould and rot, they can actually be dangerous for bees. I didn't realise this when I bought some cheap insect hotels from the shops, thinking I was doing my part for the environment.

I decided to make my own bee house, which would have removable parts to make it easier to clean and check for mites. Pollen mites are one of the biggest threats for bees. The mites eat the pollen that the bees use to feed their young, and they can also latch onto bees to get to the closest flower!

Here, I'll lead you through the steps to creating a safe bee house. I'll also tell you about some bee-friendly flowering plants that will attract them to your garden, give them food to eat and promote pollination.

What you need

Outdoor timber or recycled wood
Measuring tape and pencil
A saw
Wood glue and outdoor screws
A drill
Square blocks or logs
Chicken wire
A wire cutter

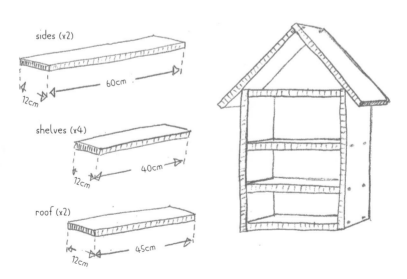

sides (x2) — 60cm — 12cm

shelves (x4) — 40cm — 12cm

roof (x2) — 45cm — 12cm

- The wood I used was 4¾ in (12 cm) wide. Choose wood that can withstand the weathers, as we don't want the bee house to rot.

- Use your measuring tape to measure the wood for the frame. I cut two side pieces to 23 ½ in (60 cm); the top and bottom pieces and two shelves to 16 in (40 cm); and the two 'roof' pieces to 17 ½ in (45 cm). Carefully cut the wood pieces and assemble them using both wood glue and screws.

- I used thick blocks of wood inside the hotel, cut to size and drilled with holes for the nesting tunnels. To encourage an equal balance between male and female bees, I drilled holes with a depth of both 4 in (10 cm) and 6 in (15 cm). If you wish, you can line your tunnels with paper straws to make them easier to clean at the end of the season.

- I also used logs from my garden and cut them to size. You can use bamboo but bear in mind that it takes longer to dry and therefore can cause mould.

- I covered the front of my bee house with wire, which I secured with screws. I have lots of bird feeders in my garden, so I wanted to deter the birds from picking at my bee hotel. Most birds prefer to eat slow-moving insects rather than bees, but check what birds are in your area and if they are a threat to your bee hotel.

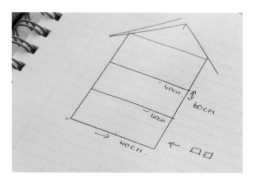

- The back of my bee hotel is open, as it is attached to a wall. This makes it easy to clean in winter, as I can lift it off the wall and remove damaged blocks from inside. If you are not securing your bee house to a wall, add some wire to the back to stop the nesting blocks from falling out. You can unscrew the back piece of wire when you need to clean the bee house.

- When positioning your bee house, place it in a sunny south-facing spot, at least one metre off the ground and clear of shrubs and vegetation. Make sure it is secure and not swinging from a tree – bees prefer to live in a solid and sturdy home.

- Keep in mind that it can take a while for bees to come to your new hotel. I positioned mine in my back garden, which has lots of wildflower buckets and bee-friendly plants. A natural way to bait the bees is to rub your bee house with a lemon balm plant – they love the scent.

Here are some bee- and butterfly-friendly flowering plants that you can plant in your garden. These provide nourishment and encourage pollination, so including them among your blooms is a great way to help the local environment.

- **Bee balm:** Also known as wild bergamot, bee balm has an attractive, aromatic flower that attracts pollinators. These plants prefer a sunnier part of your lawn and bloom during the spring and summer.

- **Foxgloves:** These tall, slender, multi-flowering plants are always surrounded by bumblebees. The tubular shape of the flower makes it easy for bees to crawl inside and get to the nectar. They collect pollen from the flower at the same time, which is used to feed the younger bees. Foxgloves are biennial, which means they will flower every second year.

- **Bluebells:** These lovely flowers bloom in early spring and are constantly surrounded by bees, butterflies and hoverflies.

- **Rosemary:** Bees love to suck nectar from rosemary flowers, so not only is it good in the kitchen, it's good in the garden too.

- **Cosmos:** These simple-looking flowers give the bees an easy route to their nectar, so they are one of the best annual bedding plants for bees. They are also very easy to grow from seed.

- **Lupine:** This bee-friendly plant produces tall, spiky flowers in late spring. Lupines love the sun, so make sure to place them in the sunniest part of the garden.

- **Lavender:** One of my favourite plants in the garden, lavender smells delicious and the bees adore it too. I have some lavender shrubs in my border and some in pots, and they are always swarming with bees when they are in flower. You can dry your lavender and use it for other projects in this book.

Sewing Terminology

- **Basting:** Also known as tacking. A basting stitch is a temporary long stitch that you can remove. Commonly used in dressmaking or sewing projects where you need to put in a temporary stitch before you do your final stitch.

- **Bias:** Bias cut simply means cutting the fabric at a 45-degree angle to the straight grain. To put it simply, fabric is cut at a diagonal angle. Fabric that is cut on the bias has more stretch and give to it. Every piece of woven fabric has two biases, perpendicular to each other. Non-woven fabrics such as felt or interfacing do not have a bias.

- **Bias binding:** Also known as binding tape. Bias binding can be handmade or you can purchase it in strips from the shop. Bias binding can be used for piping, finishing necklines and armholes, bunting and more. It is a narrow strip of fabric that has been cut on the bias and it has more stretch, making it great for finishing curved items like necklines.

- **Binding:** To finish an edge, seam or hem of a garment.

- **Casing:** A casing is a tunnel you create to allow elastic/cord to be pulled through. For example, you would create a casing for a drawstring bag or an elastic waist skirt.

- **Dart:** A dart is used to shape fabric, most often in dressmaking but also in bag-making and small crafts. In dressmaking; darts are commonly used around the bust and waist area.

- **Face:** The front-facing side, also known as the 'right side', is the patterned side of your fabric. Most fabrics have a distinct front and back. The front or right side is the side you want to be facing out when you complete your project.

- **Facing:** Fabric used to finish off the raw edge of a garment. It's similar to bias tape, but shaped facings are cut to match the edge they will face while bias facings are fabric strips cut on the bias and shaped to fit the edge.

- **Fusible interfacing:** This is an interfacing fabric with glue on one or both sides, which provides structure when it is ironed onto fabric. For example, you would use interfacing when sewing a handbag to stiffen the fabric to hold its shape.

- **Grain:** The vertical grainline runs parallel to the selvedge. The crosswise grain is at a 90-degree angle from your lengthwise grain that runs along your selvedge. The true bias grain is 45 degrees from your selvedge. Fabric cut on the true bias grain will have more stretch in it. When using a sewing pattern, you may be instructed to line up the arrow to the grain line. This is the horizontal line that is parallel to the selvedge.

- **Hem:** The folded edge of a piece of clothing. In other words, it is when you turn under and sew the edge of a piece of clothing. For example, your trousers, sleeve or dress would have a hem on the bottom.

- **Notions:** Any small tools you need for your project. On the back of a sewing pattern, there will be details on how much fabric to purchase as well as notions. These could be buttons, zips, thread etc.

- **Pattern:** A template that you can copy from. You can get many different patterns, from dressmaking patterns to patterns for household items. Most patterns are printed on tissue paper and come in a packet with instructions for you to follow. You can also create your own patterns.

- **Right side:** The right side of a piece of fabric is the printed or front side. You may be instructed to sew your right sides facing together, and this means you sew the two patterned pieces together.

- **Seam:** A seam is a line where two pieces of fabric are held together by a thread. So your hem is the fabric that is folded under, and the stitching is your seam.

- **Seam allowance:** Your seam allowance is the area between the edge of your fabric and your line of stitching. If you sew too close to the edge, your seam may be weaker and unravel. Your seam allowance can range from ¼ inch (☐ cm) to ⅝ inch (1½ cm) in most commercial patterns. You can use the throat plate on your sewing machine or a magnetic seam guide to help you with your seam allowance.

- **Selvedge or Selvage:** The tightly woven edge of your fabric. When you purchase fabric, you may notice the selvedge as it can have numbers on it. It is very difficult to fray and runs parallel to the vertical grain line.

- **Topstitch:** A topstitch is a line of stitching that is designed to be seen on the right side of your fabric. Most common on necklines and hems.

- **Wrong side:** The wrong side of your fabric is the opposite side to the patterned or right side of your fabric. It is the back of your piece of fabric.

All about Paint

- **Primer:** A primer gives your piece of furniture or surface a solid foundation for the topcoat to stick to. If you apply paint without priming, it could peel, chip and lift easily. Many special primers on the market will offer adhesion to different surfaces: tiles, metal, etc.

- **Undercoat:** If you're painting over an old layer of paint, you can use an undercoat instead of a primer. The undercoat can be especially helpful when taking the surface from dark to light. It means you will have to do fewer coats of topcoat, and it can also act as a minor filler and create a smooth base. Both primers and undercoats have a matt, chalky feel.

- **Topcoat:** This is the paint you use for the final layer. Topcoat comes in different finishes, which I will explain below. I generally apply one layer of primer and two layers of topcoat, with the topcoat in my choice of colour for the project.

Paint finishes: What texture and effect do you want?

- **Chalk paint:** Chalk paint has excellent adhesion and is great if you want an aged, French effect. Some brands market their chalk paint as a 'no-prep' paint, so you can apply it directly to wood without priming; however, the piece will need sealing with wax and varnish. It's always worth doing your prep – see page 118 for tips.

- **Eggshell:** Eggshell gives a low sheen finish. It will be self-sealing, so there's no need to apply varnish on top. It's tough and wipeable so perfect for kitchen cabinets and high-traffic areas.

- **Gloss:** This paint has a high sheen finish and is very durable and hardwearing. It's mainly used for doors and skirting boards as it's easily cleaned. Like satin and eggshell, it is self-sealing and won't require varnish.

- **Satin:** Satin sits between eggshell and gloss. It has a lower sheen finish than a gloss and once you have applied two coats, you don't need to apply varnish over it. Like eggshell, satin is durable and easy to clean.

My personal preference is for either satin or eggshell. I like the look of chalk paint but find that it doesn't wear well over time, and gloss is just too shiny for me. Satin gives a nice sprayed feel and with proper prep, it will wear well. There is no right or wrong, and it is good to have an open mind when choosing paint. Paint brands have loads of information on their websites, but if you're struggling to decide, have a chat to a stockist – not knowing which paint to pick is common, so don't be afraid to ask.

Index

Also available from The O'Brien Press

obrien.ie

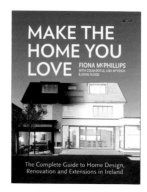

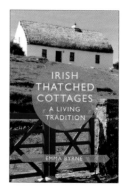

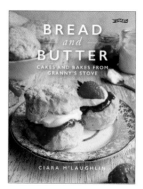